FREE Study Skills Videos/.

Dear Customer,

Thank you for your purchase from Mometrix! We consider it an honor and a privilege that you have purchased our product and we want to ensure your satisfaction.

As a way of showing our appreciation and to help us better serve you, we have developed Study Skills Videos that we would like to give you for FREE. These videos cover our *best practices* for getting ready for your exam, from how to use our study materials to how to best prepare for the day of the test.

All that we ask is that you email us with feedback that would describe your experience so far with our product. Good, bad, or indifferent, we want to know what you think!

To get your FREE Study Skills Videos, you can use the **QR code** below, or send us an **email** at studyvideos@mometrix.com with *FREE VIDEOS* in the subject line and the following information in the body of the email:

- The name of the product you purchased.
- Your product rating on a scale of 1-5, with 5 being the highest rating.
- Your feedback. It can be long, short, or anything in between. We just want to know your impressions and experience so far with our product. (Good feedback might include how our study material met your needs and ways we might be able to make it even better. You could highlight features that you found helpful or features that you think we should add.)

If you have any questions or concerns, please don't hesitate to contact me directly.

Thanks again!

Sincerely,

Jay Willis
Vice President
jay.willis@mometrix.com
1-800-673-8175

ISEE
Lower Level

Test Prep Secrets Study Guide for the Independent School Entrance Exam

Practice Questions for Math, Vocabulary, and Reading

Step-by-Step Video Tutorials

2nd Edition

Written and edited by Matthew Bowling

Printed in the United States of America

This paper meets the requirements of ANSI/NISO Z39.48-1992 (Permanence of Paper).

Mometrix offers volume discount pricing to institutions. For more information or a price quote, please contact our sales department at sales@mometrix.com or 888-248-1219.

Mometrix Media LLC is not affiliated with or endorsed by any official testing organization. All organizational and test names are trademarks of their respective owners.

Paperback
ISBN 13: 978-1-5167-1875-7
ISBN 10: 1-5167-1875-5

DEAR FUTURE EXAM SUCCESS STORY

First of all, **THANK YOU** for purchasing Mometrix study materials!

Second, congratulations! You are one of the few determined test-takers who are committed to doing whatever it takes to excel on your exam. **You have come to the right place.** We developed these study materials with one goal in mind: to deliver you the information you need in a format that's concise and easy to use.

In addition to optimizing your guide for the content of the test, we've outlined our recommended steps for breaking down the preparation process into small, attainable goals so you can make sure you stay on track.

We've also analyzed the entire test-taking process, identifying the most common pitfalls and showing how you can overcome them and be ready for any curveball the test throws you.

Standardized testing is one of the biggest obstacles on your road to success, which only increases the importance of doing well in the high-pressure, high-stakes environment of test day. Your results on this test could have a significant impact on your future, and this guide provides the information and practical advice to help you achieve your full potential on test day.

Your success is our success

We would love to hear from you! If you would like to share the story of your exam success or if you have any questions or comments in regard to our products, please contact us at **800-673-8175** or **support@mometrix.com**.

Thanks again for your business and we wish you continued success!

Sincerely,
The Mometrix Test Preparation Team

Need more help? Check out our flashcards at:
http://MometrixFlashcards.com/ISEE

TABLE OF CONTENTS

INTRODUCTION _____ 1

SECRET KEY #1 – PLAN BIG, STUDY SMALL _____ 2

SECRET KEY #2 – MAKE YOUR STUDYING COUNT _____ 3

SECRET KEY #3 – PRACTICE THE RIGHT WAY _____ 4

SECRET KEY #4 – PACE YOURSELF _____ 6

SECRET KEY #5 – HAVE A PLAN FOR GUESSING _____ 7

TEST-TAKING STRATEGIES _____ 10

VERBAL REASONING _____ 15
    SYNONYMS _____ 15
    SENTENCE COMPLETION _____ 16

MATHEMATICS _____ 18
    NUMBER SENSE _____ 18
    OPERATIONS AND PROPERTIES _____ 20
    ROUNDING AND ESTIMATION _____ 22
    DECIMALS, FRACTIONS, AND PERCENTS _____ 24
    RATIOS, PROPORTIONS, AND SCALE DRAWINGS _____ 27
    ALGEBRA, FUNCTIONS, AND PATTERNS _____ 28
    GEOMETRY _____ 32
    MEASUREMENT _____ 42
    DATA ANALYSIS AND PROBABILITY _____ 46

READING COMPREHENSION _____ 50
    READING AND THINKING _____ 50
    BUILDING A VOCABULARY _____ 55
    FIGURATIVE LANGUAGE _____ 56

ESSAY _____ 58

PRACTICE TEST _____ 62
    SECTION 1 – VERBAL REASONING _____ 62
    SECTION 2 – QUANTITATIVE REASONING _____ 67
    SECTION 3 – READING COMPREHENSION _____ 77
    SECTION 4 – MATHEMATICS ACHIEVEMENT _____ 84
    SECTION 5 – ESSAY _____ 92

ANSWERS AND EXPLANATIONS _____ 93
    SECTION 1: VERBAL REASONING _____ 93
    SECTION 2: QUANTITATIVE REASONING _____ 96
    SECTION 3: READING COMPREHENSION _____ 100
    SECTION 4: MATHEMATICS ACHIEVEMENT _____ 102

HOW TO OVERCOME TEST ANXIETY _____ 106
    CAUSES OF TEST ANXIETY _____ 106

ELEMENTS OF TEST ANXIETY _____ 107

EFFECTS OF TEST ANXIETY _____ 107

PHYSICAL STEPS FOR BEATING TEST ANXIETY _____ 108

MENTAL STEPS FOR BEATING TEST ANXIETY _____ 109

STUDY STRATEGY _____ 110

TEST TIPS _____ 112

IMPORTANT QUALIFICATION _____ 113

HOW TO OVERCOME YOUR FEAR OF MATH _____ 114

FALSE BELIEFS _____ 115

MATH STRATEGIES _____ 117

TEACHING TIPS _____ 119

SELF-CHECK _____ 120

TELL US YOUR STORY _____ 121

ADDITIONAL BONUS MATERIAL _____ 122

Introduction

Thank you for purchasing this resource! You have made the choice to prepare yourself for a test that could have a huge impact on your future, and this guide is designed to help you be fully ready for test day. Obviously, it's important to have a solid understanding of the test material, but you also need to be prepared for the unique environment and stressors of the test, so that you can perform to the best of your abilities.

For this purpose, the first section that appears in this guide is the **Secret Keys**. We've devoted countless hours to meticulously researching what works and what doesn't, and we've boiled down our findings to the five most impactful steps you can take to improve your performance on the test. We start at the beginning with study planning and move through the preparation process, all the way to the testing strategies that will help you get the most out of what you know when you're finally sitting in front of the test.

We recommend that you start preparing for your test as far in advance as possible. However, if you've bought this guide as a last-minute study resource and only have a few days before your test, we recommend that you skip over the first two Secret Keys since they address a long-term study plan.

If you struggle with **test anxiety**, we strongly encourage you to check out our recommendations for how you can overcome it. Test anxiety is a formidable foe, but it can be beaten, and we want to make sure you have the tools you need to defeat it.

Secret Key #1 – Plan Big, Study Small

There's a lot riding on your performance. If you want to ace this test, you're going to need to keep your skills sharp and the material fresh in your mind. You need a plan that lets you review everything you need to know while still fitting in your schedule. We'll break this strategy down into three categories.

Information Organization

Start with the information you already have: the official test outline. From this, you can make a complete list of all the concepts you need to cover before the test. Organize these concepts into groups that can be studied together, and create a list of any related vocabulary you need to learn so you can brush up on any difficult terms. You'll want to keep this vocabulary list handy once you actually start studying since you may need to add to it along the way.

Time Management

Once you have your set of study concepts, decide how to spread them out over the time you have left before the test. Break your study plan into small, clear goals so you have a manageable task for each day and know exactly what you're doing. Then just focus on one small step at a time. When you manage your time this way, you don't need to spend hours at a time studying. Studying a small block of content for a short period each day helps you retain information better and avoid stressing over how much you have left to do. You can relax knowing that you have a plan to cover everything in time. In order for this strategy to be effective though, you have to start studying early and stick to your schedule. Avoid the exhaustion and futility that comes from last-minute cramming!

Study Environment

The environment you study in has a big impact on your learning. Studying in a coffee shop, while probably more enjoyable, is not likely to be as fruitful as studying in a quiet room. It's important to keep distractions to a minimum. You're only planning to study for a short block of time, so make the most of it. Don't pause to check your phone or get up to find a snack. It's also important to **avoid multitasking**. Research has consistently shown that multitasking will make your studying dramatically less effective. Your study area should also be comfortable and well-lit so you don't have the distraction of straining your eyes or sitting on an uncomfortable chair.

 The time of day you study is also important. You want to be rested and alert. Don't wait until just before bedtime. Study when you'll be most likely to comprehend and remember. Even better, if you know what time of day your test will be, set that time aside for study. That way your brain will be used to working on that subject at that specific time and you'll have a better chance of recalling information.

Finally, it can be helpful to team up with others who are studying for the same test. Your actual studying should be done in as isolated an environment as possible, but the work of organizing the information and setting up the study plan can be divided up. In between study sessions, you can discuss with your teammates the concepts that you're all studying and quiz each other on the details. Just be sure that your teammates are as serious about the test as you are. If you find that your study time is being replaced with social time, you might need to find a new team.

Secret Key #2 – Make Your Studying Count

You're devoting a lot of time and effort to preparing for this test, so you want to be absolutely certain it will pay off. This means doing more than just reading the content and hoping you can remember it on test day. It's important to make every minute of study count. There are two main areas you can focus on to make your studying count.

Retention

It doesn't matter how much time you study if you can't remember the material. You need to make sure you are retaining the concepts. To check your retention of the information you're learning, try recalling it at later times with minimal prompting. Try carrying around flashcards and glance at one or two from time to time or ask a friend who's also studying for the test to quiz you.

To enhance your retention, look for ways to put the information into practice so that you can apply it rather than simply recalling it. If you're using the information in practical ways, it will be much easier to remember. Similarly, it helps to solidify a concept in your mind if you're not only reading it to yourself but also explaining it to someone else. Ask a friend to let you teach them about a concept you're a little shaky on (or speak aloud to an imaginary audience if necessary). As you try to summarize, define, give examples, and answer your friend's questions, you'll understand the concepts better and they will stay with you longer. Finally, step back for a big picture view and ask yourself how each piece of information fits with the whole subject. When you link the different concepts together and see them working together as a whole, it's easier to remember the individual components.

Finally, practice showing your work on any multi-step problems, even if you're just studying. Writing out each step you take to solve a problem will help solidify the process in your mind, and you'll be more likely to remember it during the test.

Modality

Modality simply refers to the means or method by which you study. Choosing a study modality that fits your own individual learning style is crucial. No two people learn best in exactly the same way, so it's important to know your strengths and use them to your advantage.

For example, if you learn best by visualization, focus on visualizing a concept in your mind and draw an image or a diagram. Try color-coding your notes, illustrating them, or creating symbols that will trigger your mind to recall a learned concept. If you learn best by hearing or discussing information, find a study partner who learns the same way or read aloud to yourself. Think about how to put the information in your own words. Imagine that you are giving a lecture on the topic and record yourself so you can listen to it later.

For any learning style, flashcards can be helpful. Organize the information so you can take advantage of spare moments to review. Underline key words or phrases. Use different colors for different categories. Mnemonic devices (such as creating a short list in which every item starts with the same letter) can also help with retention. Find what works best for you and use it to store the information in your mind most effectively and easily.

3

Secret Key #3 – Practice the Right Way

Your success on test day depends not only on how many hours you put into preparing, but also on whether you prepared the right way. It's good to check along the way to see if your studying is paying off. One of the most effective ways to do this is by taking practice tests to evaluate your progress. Practice tests are useful because they show exactly where you need to improve. Every time you take a practice test, pay special attention to these three groups of questions:

- The questions you got wrong
- The questions you had to guess on, even if you guessed right
- The questions you found difficult or slow to work through

This will show you exactly what your weak areas are, and where you need to devote more study time. Ask yourself why each of these questions gave you trouble. Was it because you didn't understand the material? Was it because you didn't remember the vocabulary? Do you need more repetitions on this type of question to build speed and confidence? Dig into those questions and figure out how you can strengthen your weak areas as you go back to review the material.

 Additionally, many practice tests have a section explaining the answer choices. It can be tempting to read the explanation and think that you now have a good understanding of the concept. However, an explanation likely only covers part of the question's broader context. Even if the explanation makes perfect sense, **go back and investigate** every concept related to the question until you're positive you have a thorough understanding.

As you go along, keep in mind that the practice test is just that: practice. Memorizing these questions and answers will not be very helpful on the actual test because it is unlikely to have any of the same exact questions. If you only know the right answers to the sample questions, you won't be prepared for the real thing. **Study the concepts** until you understand them fully, and then you'll be able to answer any question that shows up on the test.

It's important to wait on the practice tests until you're ready. If you take a test on your first day of study, you may be overwhelmed by the amount of material covered and how much you need to learn. Work up to it gradually.

On test day, you'll need to be prepared for answering questions, managing your time, and using the test-taking strategies you've learned. It's a lot to balance, like a mental marathon that will have a big impact on your future. Like training for a marathon, you'll need to start slowly and work your way up. When test day arrives, you'll be ready.

Start with the strategies you've read in the first two Secret Keys—plan your course and study in the way that works best for you. If you have time, consider using multiple study resources to get different approaches to the same concepts. It can be helpful to see difficult concepts from more than one angle. Then find a good source for practice tests. Many times, the test website will suggest potential study resources or provide sample tests.

Practice Test Strategy

If you're able to find at least three practice tests, we recommend this strategy:

UNTIMED AND OPEN-BOOK PRACTICE

Take the first test with no time constraints and with your notes and study guide handy. Take your time and focus on applying the strategies you've learned.

TIMED AND OPEN-BOOK PRACTICE

Take the second practice test open-book as well, but set a timer and practice pacing yourself to finish in time.

TIMED AND CLOSED-BOOK PRACTICE

Take any other practice tests as if it were test day. Set a timer and put away your study materials. Sit at a table or desk in a quiet room, imagine yourself at the testing center, and answer questions as quickly and accurately as possible.

Keep repeating timed and closed-book tests on a regular basis until you run out of practice tests or it's time for the actual test. Your mind will be ready for the schedule and stress of test day, and you'll be able to focus on recalling the material you've learned.

Secret Key #4 – Pace Yourself

Once you're fully prepared for the material on the test, your biggest challenge on test day will be managing your time. Just knowing that the clock is ticking can make you panic even if you have plenty of time left. Work on pacing yourself so you can build confidence against the time constraints of the exam. Pacing is a difficult skill to master, especially in a high-pressure environment, so **practice is vital**.

Set time expectations for your pace based on how much time is available. For example, if a section has 60 questions and the time limit is 30 minutes, you know you have to average 30 seconds or less per question in order to answer them all. Although 30 seconds is the hard limit, set 25 seconds per question as your goal, so you reserve extra time to spend on harder questions. When you budget extra time for the harder questions, you no longer have any reason to stress when those questions take longer to answer.

Don't let this time expectation distract you from working through the test at a calm, steady pace, but keep it in mind so you don't spend too much time on any one question. Recognize that taking extra time on one question you don't understand may keep you from answering two that you do understand later in the test. If your time limit for a question is up and you're still not sure of the answer, mark it and move on, and come back to it later if the time and the test format allow. If the testing format doesn't allow you to return to earlier questions, just make an educated guess; then put it out of your mind and move on.

On the easier questions, be careful not to rush. It may seem wise to hurry through them so you have more time for the challenging ones, but it's not worth missing one if you know the concept and just didn't take the time to read the question fully. Work efficiently but make sure you understand the question and have looked at all of the answer choices, since more than one may seem right at first.

Even if you're paying attention to the time, you may find yourself a little behind at some point. You should speed up to get back on track, but do so wisely. Don't panic; just take a few seconds less on each question until you're caught up. Don't guess without thinking, but do look through the answer choices and eliminate any you know are wrong. If you can get down to two choices, it is often worthwhile to guess from those. Once you've chosen an answer, move on and don't dwell on any that you skipped or had to hurry through. If a question was taking too long, chances are it was one of the harder ones, so you weren't as likely to get it right anyway.

On the other hand, if you find yourself getting ahead of schedule, it may be beneficial to slow down a little. The more quickly you work, the more likely you are to make a careless mistake that will affect your score. You've budgeted time for each question, so don't be afraid to spend that time. Practice an efficient but careful pace to get the most out of the time you have.

Secret Key #5 – Have a Plan for Guessing

When you're taking the test, you may find yourself stuck on a question. Some of the answer choices seem better than others, but you don't see the one answer choice that is obviously correct. What do you do?

The scenario described above is very common, yet most test takers have not effectively prepared for it. Developing and practicing a plan for guessing may be one of the single most effective uses of your time as you get ready for the exam.

In developing your plan for guessing, there are three questions to address:

- When should you start the guessing process?
- How should you narrow down the choices?
- Which answer should you choose?

When to Start the Guessing Process

Unless your plan for guessing is to select C every time (which, despite its merits, is not what we recommend), you need to leave yourself enough time to apply your answer elimination strategies. Since you have a limited amount of time for each question, that means that if you're going to give yourself the best shot at guessing correctly, you have to decide quickly whether or not you will guess.

Of course, the best-case scenario is that you don't have to guess at all, so first, see if you can answer the question based on your knowledge of the subject and basic reasoning skills. Focus on the key words in the question and try to jog your memory of related topics. Give yourself a chance to bring the knowledge to mind, but once you realize that you don't have (or you can't access) the knowledge you need to answer the question, it's time to start the guessing process.

It's almost always better to start the guessing process too early than too late. It only takes a few seconds to remember something and answer the question from knowledge. Carefully eliminating wrong answer choices takes longer. Plus, going through the process of eliminating answer choices can actually help jog your memory.

Summary: Start the guessing process as soon as you decide that you can't answer the question based on your knowledge.

7

How to Narrow Down the Choices

The next chapter in this book (**Test-Taking Strategies**) includes a wide range of strategies for how to approach questions and how to look for answer choices to eliminate. You will definitely want to read those carefully, practice them, and figure out which ones work best for you. Here though, we're going to address a mindset rather than a particular strategy.

Your odds of guessing an answer correctly depend on how many options you are choosing from.

Number of options left	5	4	3	2	1
Odds of guessing correctly	20%	25%	33%	50%	100%

You can see from this chart just how valuable it is to be able to eliminate incorrect answers and make an educated guess, but there are two things that many test takers do that cause them to miss out on the benefits of guessing:

- Accidentally eliminating the correct answer
- Selecting an answer based on an impression

We'll look at the first one here, and the second one in the next section.

To avoid accidentally eliminating the correct answer, we recommend a thought exercise called **the $5 challenge**. In this challenge, you only eliminate an answer choice from contention if you are willing to bet $5 on it being wrong. Why $5? Five dollars is a small but not insignificant amount of money. It's an amount you could afford to lose but wouldn't want to throw away. And while losing

$5 once might not hurt too much, doing it twenty times will set you back $100. In the same way, each small decision you make—eliminating a choice here, guessing on a question there—won't by itself impact your score very much, but when you put them all together, they can make a big difference. By holding each answer choice elimination decision to a higher standard, you can reduce the risk of accidentally eliminating the correct answer.

The $5 challenge can also be applied in a positive sense: If you are willing to bet $5 that an answer choice *is* correct, go ahead and mark it as correct.

Summary: Only eliminate an answer choice if you are willing to bet $5 that it is wrong.

Which Answer to Choose

You're taking the test. You've run into a hard question and decided you'll have to guess. You've eliminated all the answer choices you're willing to bet $5 on. Now you have to pick an answer. Why do we even need to talk about this? Why can't you just pick whichever one you feel like when the time comes?

The answer to these questions is that if you don't come into the test with a plan, you'll rely on your impression to select an answer choice, and if you do that, you risk falling into a trap. The test writers know that everyone who takes their test will be guessing on some of the questions, so they intentionally write wrong answer choices to seem plausible. You still have to pick an answer though, and if the wrong answer choices are designed to look right, how can you ever be sure that you're not falling for their trap? The best solution we've found to this dilemma is to take the decision out of your hands entirely. Here is the process we recommend:

Once you've eliminated any choices that you are confident (willing to bet $5) are wrong, select the first remaining choice as your answer.

Whether you choose to select the first remaining choice, the second, or the last, the important thing is that you use some preselected standard. Using this approach guarantees that you will not be enticed into selecting an answer choice that looks right, because you are not basing your decision on how the answer choices look.

This is not meant to make you question your knowledge. Instead, it is to help you recognize the difference between your knowledge and your impressions. There's a huge difference between thinking an answer is right because of what you know, and thinking an answer is right because it looks or sounds like it should be right.

Summary: To ensure that your selection is appropriately random, make a predetermined selection from among all answer choices you have not eliminated.

Test-Taking Strategies

This section contains a list of test-taking strategies that you may find helpful as you work through the test. By taking what you know and applying logical thought, you can maximize your chances of answering any question correctly!

It is very important to realize that every question is different and every person is different: no single strategy will work on every question, and no single strategy will work for every person. That's why we've included all of them here, so you can try them out and determine which ones work best for different types of questions and which ones work best for you.

Question Strategies

✓ READ CAREFULLY

Read the question and the answer choices carefully. Don't miss the question because you misread the terms. You have plenty of time to read each question thoroughly and make sure you understand what is being asked. Yet a happy medium must be attained, so don't waste too much time. You must read carefully and efficiently.

✓ CONTEXTUAL CLUES

Look for contextual clues. If the question includes a word you are not familiar with, look at the immediate context for some indication of what the word might mean. Contextual clues can often give you all the information you need to decipher the meaning of an unfamiliar word. Even if you can't determine the meaning, you may be able to narrow down the possibilities enough to make a solid guess at the answer to the question.

✓ PREFIXES

If you're having trouble with a word in the question or answer choices, try dissecting it. Take advantage of every clue that the word might include. Prefixes and suffixes can be a huge help. Usually, they allow you to determine a basic meaning. *Pre-* means before, *post-* means after, *pro-* is positive, *de-* is negative. From prefixes and suffixes, you can get an idea of the general meaning of the word and try to put it into context.

✓ HEDGE WORDS

Watch out for critical hedge words, such as *likely, may, can, sometimes, often, almost, mostly, usually, generally, rarely,* and *sometimes.* Question writers insert these hedge phrases to cover every possibility. Often an answer choice will be wrong simply because it leaves no room for exception. Be on guard for answer choices that have definitive words such as *exactly* and *always.*

✓ SWITCHBACK WORDS

Stay alert for *switchbacks*. These are the words and phrases frequently used to alert you to shifts in thought. The most common switchback words are *but, although,* and *however.* Others include *nevertheless, on the other hand, even though, while, in spite of, despite,* and *regardless of.* Switchback words are important to catch because they can change the direction of the question or an answer choice.

10

⏀ Face Value

When in doubt, use common sense. Accept the situation in the problem at face value. Don't read too much into it. These problems will not require you to make wild assumptions. If you have to go beyond creativity and warp time or space in order to have an answer choice fit the question, then you should move on and consider the other answer choices. These are normal problems rooted in reality. The applicable relationship or explanation may not be readily apparent, but it is there for you to figure out. Use your common sense to interpret anything that isn't clear.

Answer Choice Strategies

⏀ Answer Selection

The most thorough way to pick an answer choice is to identify and eliminate wrong answers until only one is left, then confirm it is the correct answer. Sometimes an answer choice may immediately seem right, but be careful. The test writers will usually put more than one reasonable answer choice on each question, so take a second to read all of them and make sure that the other choices are not equally obvious. As long as you have time left, it is better to read every answer choice than to pick the first one that looks right without checking the others.

⏀ Answer Choice Families

An answer choice family consists of two (in rare cases, three) answer choices that are very similar in construction and cannot all be true at the same time. If you see two answer choices that are direct opposites or parallels, one of them is usually the correct answer. For instance, if one answer choice says that quantity x increases and another either says that quantity x decreases (opposite) or says that quantity y increases (parallel), then those answer choices would fall into the same family. An answer choice that doesn't match the construction of the answer choice family is more likely to be incorrect. Most questions will not have answer choice families, but when they do appear, you should be prepared to recognize them.

⏀ Eliminate Answers

Eliminate answer choices as soon as you realize they are wrong, but make sure you consider all possibilities. If you are eliminating answer choices and realize that the last one you are left with is also wrong, don't panic. Start over and consider each choice again. There may be something you missed the first time that you will realize on the second pass.

⏀ Avoid Fact Traps

Don't be distracted by an answer choice that is factually true but doesn't answer the question. You are looking for the choice that answers the question. Stay focused on what the question is asking for so you don't accidentally pick an answer that is true but incorrect. Always go back to the question and make sure the answer choice you've selected actually answers the question and is not merely a true statement.

⏀ Extreme Statements

In general, you should avoid answers that put forth extreme actions as standard practice or proclaim controversial ideas as established fact. An answer choice that states the "process should be used in certain situations, if..." is much more likely to be correct than one that states the "process should be discontinued completely." The first is a calm rational statement and doesn't even make a definitive, uncompromising stance, using a hedge word *if* to provide wiggle room, whereas the second choice is far more extreme.

⊘ BENCHMARK

As you read through the answer choices and you come across one that seems to answer the question well, mentally select that answer choice. This is not your final answer, but it's the one that will help you evaluate the other answer choices. The one that you selected is your benchmark or standard for judging each of the other answer choices. Every other answer choice must be compared to your benchmark. That choice is correct until proven otherwise by another answer choice beating it. If you find a better answer, then that one becomes your new benchmark. Once you've decided that no other choice answers the question as well as your benchmark, you have your final answer.

⊘ PREDICT THE ANSWER

Before you even start looking at the answer choices, it is often best to try to predict the answer. When you come up with the answer on your own, it is easier to avoid distractions and traps because you will know exactly what to look for. The right answer choice is unlikely to be word-for-word what you came up with, but it should be a close match. Even if you are confident that you have the right answer, you should still take the time to read each option before moving on.

General Strategies

⊘ TOUGH QUESTIONS

If you are stumped on a problem or it appears too hard or too difficult, don't waste time. Move on! Remember though, if you can quickly check for obviously incorrect answer choices, your chances of guessing correctly are greatly improved. Before you completely give up, at least try to knock out a couple of possible answers. Eliminate what you can and then guess at the remaining answer choices before moving on.

⊘ CHECK YOUR WORK

Since you will probably not know every term listed and the answer to every question, it is important that you get credit for the ones that you do know. Don't miss any questions through careless mistakes. If at all possible, try to take a second to look back over your answer selection and make sure you've selected the correct answer choice and haven't made a costly careless mistake (such as marking an answer choice that you didn't mean to mark). This quick double check should more than pay for itself in caught mistakes for the time it costs.

⊘ PACE YOURSELF

It's easy to be overwhelmed when you're looking at a page full of questions; your mind is confused and full of random thoughts, and the clock is ticking down faster than you would like. Calm down and maintain the pace that you have set for yourself. Especially as you get down to the last few minutes of the test, don't let the small numbers on the clock make you panic. As long as you are on track by monitoring your pace, you are guaranteed to have time for each question.

⊘ DON'T RUSH

It is very easy to make errors when you are in a hurry. Maintaining a fast pace in answering questions is pointless if it makes you miss questions that you would have gotten right otherwise. Test writers like to include distracting information and wrong answers that seem right. Taking a little extra time to avoid careless mistakes can make all the difference in your test score. Find a pace that allows you to be confident in the answers that you select.

⊘ Keep Moving

Panicking will not help you pass the test, so do your best to stay calm and keep moving. Taking deep breaths and going through the answer elimination steps you practiced can help to break through a stress barrier and keep your pace.

Final Notes

The combination of a solid foundation of content knowledge and the confidence that comes from practicing your plan for applying that knowledge is the key to maximizing your performance on test day. As your foundation of content knowledge is built up and strengthened, you'll find that the strategies included in this chapter become more and more effective in helping you quickly sift through the distractions and traps of the test to isolate the correct answer.

Now that you're preparing to move forward into the test content chapters of this book, be sure to keep your goal in mind. As you read, think about how you will be able to apply this information on the test. If you've already seen sample questions for the test and you have an idea of the question format and style, try to come up with questions of your own that you can answer based on what you're reading. This will give you valuable practice applying your knowledge in the same ways you can expect to on test day.

Good luck and good studying!

Verbal Reasoning

Synonyms

As part of your exam, you need to understand how words connect to each other. This is done with understanding words that mean the same thing or synonyms. For example, *dry* and *arid* are synonyms. There are pairs of words in English that can be called synonyms. Yet, they have somewhat different definitions.

For example, *wise* and *intelligent* can be used to describe someone who is very educated. So, you would be correct to call them synonyms. However, *wise* is used for good judgment. *Intelligent* is closer to good thinking.

Words should not be called synonyms when their differences are too great. For example, *hot* and *warm* are not synonyms because their meanings are too different. How do you know when two words are synonyms? First, try to replace one word for the other word. Then, be sure that the meaning of the sentence has not changed. Replacing *warm* for *hot* in a sentence gives a different meaning. *Warm* and *hot* may seem close in meaning. Yet, *warm* means that the temperature is normal. And, *hot* means that the temperature is very high.

> **Review Video: Synonyms and Antonyms**
> Visit mometrix.com/academy and enter code: 105612
>
> **Review Video: Synonyms**
> Visit mometrix.com/academy and enter code: 355036

SYNONYMS

For the Synonyms section, you will have one word and four choices for a synonym of that word. Before you look at the choices, try to think of a few words that could be a synonym for your question. Then, check the choices for a synonym of the question. Some words may seem close to the question, but you are looking for the best choice of a synonym. So, don't let your first reaction be your final decision.

Example 1

Precise:

> A. Focus
> B. Careless
> C. Exact
> D. Costly

Example 2

Fringe:

> A. Neglect
> B. Margin
> C. Fade
> D. Center

Example 3

Splendid:

    A. Unknown
    B. Beautiful
    C. Awkward
    D. Ordinary

ANSWERS

Example 1: C, Exact

Example 2: B, Margin

Example 3: B, Beautiful

Sentence Completion

On your exam and in everyday life, you will be introduced to unfamiliar words. Most of the time, the definition of an unknown word can be learned from context clues. Context refers to how a word or phrase is used in a sentence. Understanding the context can help you decide which word or phrase should go in the blank. There are different contextual clues such as definition, description, example, comparison, and contrast. The following are examples:

- Definition: the unknown word is clearly defined by the previous words.
  - "When he was painting, his instrument was a ___." (paintbrush)
- Description: the unknown word is described by the previous words.
  - "I was hot, tired, and thirsty; I was ___." (dehydrated)
- Example: the unknown word is part of a series of examples.
  - "Water, soda, and ___ were the offered beverages." (coffee)
- Comparison: the unknown word is compared to another word.
  - "Barney is agreeable and happy like his ___ parents." (positive)
- Contrast: the unknown word is contrasted with another word.
  - "I prefer cold weather to ___ conditions." (hot)

SENTENCE COMPLETION

The second type of question in the Verbal Reasoning section asks you to read a sentence with a missing word and fill in the blank with the appropriate word. Also, some questions will ask you to read part of a sentence, and you will need to decide how to finish the sentence. In the same way with the Synonyms section, you should read the question and think of a few possible ways to complete the sentence. Then, look over your choices and select the best choice.

Example 1

Determine how to complete this sentence:

    Danny was so _____ that his teacher had to keep reminding him to be serious.

To fill in the blank, you need to look at the context of the sentence. In this example, Danny's teacher reminds him to be serious. If the teacher has to remind Danny to be serious, then Danny must be doing the opposite. When someone is not being serious, they are being silly or causing mischief. Then, you would look over your answer choices and decide on a word that is similar to being silly or causing mischief.

Example 2

Determine how to complete this sentence:

As an actor, he _____ a king, a homeless man, and an investigator.

In this example, you know that the subject of the sentence is an actor. So, you would look over your answer choices and decide on a word that relates to acting like *portrayed* or *represented*.

Example 3

Determine how to complete this sentence:

When the commander arrived at the base, the soldiers _____.

In this example, we see the connection between soldiers and their commanding officer. You do not need to know the rules and procedures of greeting someone of a high military rank. The soldiers are not as important as the commander. So, you will be looking for an answer choice that has the soldiers showing respect to the commander. An example could be "the soldiers took their position" or "the soldiers saluted their officer."

Mathematics

Number Sense

NUMBERS AND THEIR CLASSIFICATIONS

There are several different kinds of numbers. When you learn to count as a child, you start with *Natural Numbers*. You may know them as counting numbers. These numbers begin with 1, 2, 3, and so on. *Whole Numbers* are all natural numbers and zero.

Aside from the number 1, all natural numbers are known as prime or composite. *Prime Numbers* are natural numbers that are greater than 1 and have factors that are 1 and itself (e.g., 3). On the other hand, *Composite Numbers* are natural numbers that are greater than 1 and are not prime numbers. The number 1 is a special case because it is not a prime number or composite number.

Numbers are the basic building blocks of mathematics. These terms show some elements of numbers:

Even number – Any integer that can be divided by 2 and does not leave a remainder.

Example: 2, 4, 6, 8, etc.

Odd number – Any integer that cannot be divided evenly by 2. For example: 3, 5, 7, 9, and so on.

Decimal number – a number that uses a decimal point to show the part of the number that is less than one. Example: 1.234.

Decimal point – a symbol used to separate the ones place from the tenths place in decimals. This symbol is used to separate dollars from cents in currency.

Decimal place – the position of a number to the right of the decimal point. In the decimal 0.123, the 1 is in the first place to the right of the decimal point. This is the place for tenths. The 2 is in the second place. This is the place for hundredths. The 3 is in the third place. This is the place for thousandths.

The decimal, or base 10, system is a number system that uses ten different digits (0, 1, 2, 3, 4, 5, 6, 7, 8, 9). Another system is the binary, or base 2, number system. This system is used by computers and uses the numbers 0 and 1. Some think that the base 10 system started because people had only their 10 fingers for counting.

PLACE VALUE

Write the place value of each digit in the following number: 14,059.826

1: ten thousands

4: thousands

0: hundreds

5: tens

9: ones

8: tenths

2: hundredths

6: thousandths

WRITING NUMBERS IN WORD FORM

Example 1

Write each number in words.

29: twenty-nine

478: four hundred seventy-eight

9,435: nine thousand four hundred thirty-five

98,542: ninety-eight thousand five hundred forty-two

302, 876: three hundred two thousand eight hundred seventy-six

Example 2

Write each decimal in words.

0.06: six hundredths

0.6: six tenths

6.0: six

0.009: nine thousandths

0.113: one hundred thirteen thousandths

0.901: nine hundred and one thousandths

THE NUMBER LINE

A number line is a graph to see the distance between numbers. Basically, this graph shows the relationship between numbers. So a number line may have a point for zero and may show negative numbers on the left side of the line. Also, any positive numbers are placed on the right side of the line. For example, consider the points labeled on the following number line:

19

We can use the dashed lines on the number line to identify each point. Each dashed line between two whole numbers is $\frac{1}{4}$. The line halfway between two numbers is $\frac{1}{2}$.

LISTING NUMBERS: LEAST TO GREATEST

Example 1

4,002; 280; 108,511; 9

Answer: 9; 280; 4,002; 108,511

Example 2

5,075,000,600; 190,800,330; 7,000,300,001

Answer: 190,800,330; 5,075,000,600; 7,000,300,001

Operations and Properties

OPERATIONS

There are four basic operations in math: addition, subtraction, multiplication, and division.

Addition increases the value of one number by the value of another number.

Example: 2 + 4 = 6; 8 + 9 = 17. The result is called the sum. With addition, the order does not matter. 4 + 2 or 2 + 4 equals 6. This is the commutative property for addition.

Subtraction decreases the value of one number by the value of another number. The result is called the difference. Example: 6 – 4 = 2 and 17 – 8 = 9. Note for subtraction that the order does matter. For example, 6 – 4 and 4 – 6 do not have the same difference.

Multiplication is like repeated addition. This operation tells how many times one number needs to be added to the other number. Example: 3 × 2 (three times two) = 2 + 2 + 2 = 6. With multiplication, the order does not matter. 2 × 3 (or 3 + 3) = 3 × 2 (or 2 + 2 + 2). This is the commutative property for multiplication.

Division is the opposite operation to multiplication. This operation shows how much of a number is in another number. The first number is known as the dividend. The second number is known as the divisor. The answer to the division problem is known as the quotient.

Example: 20 ÷ 4 = 5. If 20 is split into 4 equal parts, then each part is 5. With division, the order of the numbers does matter. 20 ÷ 4 and 4 ÷ 20 do not give the same result. Note that you cannot divide a number by zero. If you try to divide a number by zero, then the answer is known as undefined.

ORDER OF OPERATIONS

Order of Operations is a list of rules that gives the order of doing each operation in an expression. If you have an expression that with many different operations, Order of Operations tells you which operations to do first. An easy way to remember Order of Operations is PEMDAS.

This is written out as "Please Excuse My Dear Aunt Sally." PEMDAS stands for Parentheses, Exponents, Multiplication, Division, Addition, Subtraction. You need to understand that multiplication and division are equal as steps. Also, addition and subtraction are equal as steps. So, those pairs of operations are worked from left to right.

Example: Use order of operations for the expression $5 + 20 \div 4 \times (2 + 3)^2 - 6$.

P: Work on the operations inside the parentheses, $(2 + 3) = 5$.

E: Simplify the exponents, $(5)^2 = 25$.

The equation now looks like this: $5 + 20 \div 4 \times 25 - 6$.

MD: Work on multiplication and division from left to right, $20 \div 4 = 5$; then $5 \times 25 = 125$.

The equation now looks like this: $5 + 125 - 6$.

AS: Work on addition and subtraction from left to right, $5 + 125 = 130$; then $130 - 6 = 124$.

> **Review Video: Order of Operations**
> Visit mometrix.com/academy and enter code: 259675

PROPERTIES

The Commutative Property of Addition is shown here, which states that you can add terms in any order.

$$2x + y = y + 2x$$

The Distributive Property is shown here, which states that a number multiplied to an expression in parentheses must be multiplied to every term in the parentheses.

$$5 \times (x + 1) = (5 \times x) + (5 \times 1)$$

The Identity Property of Multiplication is shown here, which states that multiplying a number or term by 1 does not change its value.

$$3 \times 1 = 3$$

The Commutative Property of Multiplication is shown here, which states that you can multiply terms in any order.

$$6 \times m \times n = m \times n \times 6$$

The Associative Property of Multiplication is shown here, which states that any group of numbers and/or variables can be grouped together in parentheses to be multiplied first before multiplying by the remaining numbers and/or variables.

$$4 \times (5a) = (4a) \times 5$$

The Identity Property of Addition is shown here, which states that adding 0 to any number or term does not change the value of that number or term.

$$s + 0 = s$$

The Associative Property of Addition is shown here, which states that any group of numbers and/or variables can be grouped together in parentheses to be added first before adding the remaining numbers and/or variables.

$$10 + (6 + 1) = (10 + 6) + 1$$

COEFFICIENTS AND THE DISTRIBUTIVE PROPERTY

COEFFICIENTS

A coefficient is a number or symbol that is multiplied by a variable. For example, in the expression 2(ab), the number 2 is the coefficient of (ab). The expression can be written in other ways to have a different coefficient. For example, the expression can be 2a(b). This means that 2a is the coefficient of (b).

DISTRIBUTIVE PROPERTY

The distributive property can be used to multiply each addend in parentheses. Then, the products are added to reach the result. The formula for the distributive property looks like this:

$$a(b + c) = ab + ac$$

Example: 6(2+4)

First, multiply 6 and 2. The answer is 12.

Then, multiply 6 and 4. The answer is 24.

Last, we add 12 and 24. So, the final answer is 36.

Rounding and Estimation

ROUNDING

Rounding is lowering the digits in a number and keeping the value similar. The result will be less accurate. However, this will be in a simpler form and will be easier to use. Whole numbers can be rounded to the nearest ten, hundred or thousand. Also, fractions and decimals can be rounded to the nearest whole number.

Example 1

Round each number to the nearest ten: 11 | 47 | 118

When rounding to the nearest ten, anything ending in 5 or greater rounds up.

So, 11 rounds to 10 | 47 rounds to 50 | 118 rounds to 120.

Example 2

Round each number to the nearest hundred: 78 | 980 | 248

When rounding to the nearest hundred, anything ending in 50 or greater rounds up.

So, 78 rounds to 100 | 980 rounds to 1000 | 248 rounds down to 200.

Example 3

Round each number to the nearest thousand: 302 | 1274 | 3756

When rounding to the nearest thousand, anything ending in 500 or greater rounds up.

So, 302 rounds to 0 | 1274 rounds to 1000 | 3756 rounds to 4000.

Example 4

Round each number to the nearest whole number: $\frac{5}{8}$ | 2.12 | $\frac{14}{3}$

When rounding fractions and decimals, anything half or higher rounds up.

So, $\frac{5}{8}$ rounds to 1 | 2.12 rounds to 2 | $\frac{14}{3}$ rounds to 5.

ESTIMATION

Estimation is the process of finding an approximate answer to a problem. Estimation may involve rounding to the nearest whole number to make addition or subtraction easier.

Example 1

There are 24 people in an English class. Miss Foster decides to order three exam books for each student, plus 6 extras. She estimates that she should order 90 exam books. Identify if her solution is reasonable.

Write an expression to determine the total number of exam books to order. Since three books are ordered for each student, first multiply the number of books per student by the number of students: 3 books per student · 24 students = 72 books. Next, add the six extra exam books that Miss Foster would like to order. The total number of books to order is: 72 + 6 = 78 books. Her original estimate of 90 exam books is too large.

Example 2

The following food items are available in a school cafeteria for lunch:

Sandwich: $3.15; Soup: $1.84

Salad: $2.62; Pretzels: $0.95

Milk: $0.40

Daniel has $4.00 and wants to purchase a milk, sandwich, and soup. Emily has $4.00 and wants to purchase a salad, pretzels, and milk. Estimate the cost of each student's lunch and determine if they have enough money to purchase the food they would like for lunch.

Daniel wants to purchase a milk, sandwich, and soup. Rounded to the nearest fifty cents, the cost of his items is $0.50, $3.00, and $2.00. The total for his three items would be approximately:

$$0.50 + 3.00 + 2.00 = 5.50$$

It will cost Daniel approximately $5.50 for his lunch. He does not have enough money to purchase the items he has selected.

Emily wants to purchase a salad, pretzels, and milk. Rounded to the nearest fifty cents, the cost of her items is $2.50, $1.00, and $0.50. The total for her three items would be approximately:

$$2.50 + 1.00 + 0.50 = 4.00$$

It will cost Emily approximately $4.00 for her lunch. She has approximately enough money to purchase the items she has selected.

Decimals, Fractions, and Percents

DECIMALS

DECIMAL ILLUSTRATION

Use a model to represent the decimal: 0.24. Write 0.24 as a fraction. The decimal 0.24 is twenty-four hundredths. One possible model to represent this fraction is to draw 100 pennies, since each penny is worth 1 one hundredth of a dollar. Draw one hundred circles to represent one hundred pennies. Shade 24 of the pennies to represent the decimal twenty-four hundredths.

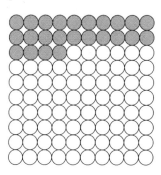

To write the decimal as a fraction, write a fraction: $\frac{\text{\# shaded spaces}}{\text{\# total spaces}}$. The number of shaded spaces is 24, and the total number of spaces is 100, so as a fraction 0.24 equals $\frac{24}{100}$. $\frac{24}{100}$ can then be reduced to $\frac{6}{25}$.

ADDING AND SUBTRACTING DECIMALS

When adding and subtracting decimals, the decimal points must always be aligned. Adding decimals is just like adding regular whole numbers.

Example: 4.5 + 2 = 6.5.

If the problem-solver does not properly align the decimal points, an incorrect answer of 4.7 may result. An easy way to add decimals is to align all of the decimal points in a vertical column visually. This will allow one to see exactly where the decimal should be placed in the final answer. Begin adding from right to left. Add each column in turn, making sure to carry the number to the left if a column adds up to more than 9. The same rules apply to the subtraction of decimals.

Review Video: Adding and Subtracting Decimals
Visit mometrix.com/academy and enter code: 381101

FRACTIONS

A fraction has one integer that is written above another integer with a dividing line between them $\left(\frac{x}{y}\right)$. It represents the quotient of the two numbers "x divided by y." Also, this can be thought of as x out of y equal parts. The x and y in this fraction are known as variables. When the value for a symbol can change, a variable is given to that value. So, a number like 3 is a constant. A value that does not change is a constant.

The top number of a fraction is called the numerator. This number stands for the number of parts. The 1 in $\frac{1}{4}$ means that this is one part out of the whole. The bottom number of a fraction is called the denominator. This stands for the total number of equal parts. The 4 in $\frac{1}{4}$ means that the whole has four equal parts. A fraction cannot have a denominator of zero. This fraction is known as "undefined." The reverse of a fraction is known as the reciprocal. For example, the reciprocal of 1/2 is 2, and the reciprocal of 3 is 1/3.

Fractions can be changed by multiplying or dividing the numerator and denominator by the same number. This will not change the value of the fraction. You cannot do this with addition or subtraction. If you divide both numbers by a common factor, you will reduce or simplify the fraction. Two fractions that have the same value but are given in different ways are known as equivalent fractions. For example, $\frac{2}{10}, \frac{3}{15}, \frac{4}{20}$, and $\frac{5}{25}$ are equivalent fractions. Also, they can be reduced or simplified to $\frac{1}{5}$.

Two fractions can be changed to have the same denominator. This is known as finding a common denominator. The number for the common denominator should be the least common multiple of the original denominators. Example: $\frac{3}{4}$ and $\frac{5}{6}$; the least common multiple of 4 and 6 is 12. So, you can change these fractions to have a common denominator: $\frac{3}{4} = \frac{9}{12}$ and $\frac{5}{6} = \frac{10}{12}$.

If two fractions have a common denominator, you can add or subtract the fractions with the two numerators. Example: $\frac{1}{2} + \frac{1}{4} = \frac{2}{4} + \frac{1}{4} = \frac{3}{4}$. If the two fractions do not have the same denominator, one or both of them must be changed to have a common denominator. This needs to be done before they can be added or subtracted.

A fraction with a denominator that is greater than the numerator is known as a proper fraction. A fraction with a numerator that is greater than the denominator is known as an improper fraction. Proper fractions have values less than one. Improper fractions have values greater than one.

A mixed number is a number that has an integer and a fraction. Any improper fraction can be rewritten as a mixed number. Example: $\frac{8}{3} = \frac{6}{3} + \frac{2}{3} = 2 + \frac{2}{3} = 2\frac{2}{3}$.

25

Copyright © Mometrix Media. You have been licensed one copy of this document for personal use only. Any other reproduction or redistribution is strictly prohibited. All rights reserved.

Also, any mixed number can be rewritten as an improper fraction. Example: $1\frac{3}{5} = 1 + \frac{3}{5} = \frac{5}{5} + \frac{3}{5} = \frac{8}{5}$.

CONVERTING DECIMALS TO FRACTIONS

A fraction can be turned into a decimal and vice versa. In order to convert a fraction into a decimal, simply divide the numerator by the denominator. For example, the fraction $\frac{5}{4}$ becomes 1.25. This is done by dividing 5 by 4. The fraction $\frac{4}{8}$ becomes 0.5 when 4 is divided by 8. This remains true even if the fraction $\frac{4}{8}$ is first reduced to $\frac{1}{2}$. The decimal conversion will still be 0.5. In order to convert a decimal into a fraction, count the number of places to the right of the decimal. This will be the number of zeros in the denominator. The numbers to the right of the decimal will become the whole number in the numerator.

<u>Example 1:</u>

$0.45 = \frac{45}{100}$

$\frac{45}{100}$ reduces to $\frac{9}{20}$

<u>Example 2:</u>

$0.237 = \frac{237}{1000}$

<u>Example 3:</u>

$0.2121 = \frac{2121}{10000}$

PERCENTAGES

You can think of percentages as fractions that are based on a whole of 100. In other words, one whole is equal to 100%. The word percent means "per hundred." Fractions can be given as percents by using equivalent fractions with an amount of 100. Example: $\frac{7}{10} = \frac{70}{100} = 70\%$; Another example is $\frac{1}{4} = \frac{25}{100} = 25\%$. To give a percentage as a fraction, divide the percentage by 100. Then, reduce the fraction to its simplest possible terms. Example: $60\% = \frac{60}{100} = \frac{3}{5}$; $96\% = \frac{96}{100} = \frac{24}{25}$.

Converting decimals to percentages and percentages to decimals is as simple as moving the decimal point. To convert from a decimal to a percent, move the decimal point two places to the right. To convert from a percent to a decimal, move the decimal two places to the left.

Example: 0.23 = 23%; 5.34 = 534%; 0.007 = 0.7%; 700% = 7.00; 86% = 0.86; 0.15% = 0.0015.

Ratios, Proportions, and Scale Drawings

RATIOS

A ratio is a comparison of two numbers in a certain order. Example: There are 14 computers in a lab, and the class has 20 students. So, there is a student to computer ratio of 20 to 14. Normally, this is written as 20:14.

Ratios can be listed as *a to b*, *a:b*, or *a/b*. Examples of ratios are miles per hour (miles/hour), meters per second (meters/second), and miles per gallon (miles/gallon).

> **Review Video: Ratios**
> Visit mometrix.com/academy and enter code: 996914

PROPORTIONS AND CROSS PRODUCTS

A proportion is a relationship between two numbers. This relationship shows how one changes when the other changes. A direct proportion is a relationship where a number increases by a set amount with every increase in the other number.

Another way is for the number to decrease by that same amount for every decrease in the other quantity. Example: For every 1 sheet cake, 18 people can have cake. The number of sheet cakes and the number of people that can be served from them is a direct proportion.

Inverse proportion is a relationship where an increase in one number has a decrease in the other. This can work the other way where a decrease in a number has an increase in the other.

Example: The time needed for a car trip decreases as the speed increases. Also, the time for the trip increases as the speed decreases. So, the time needed for the trip is inversely proportional to the speed of the car.

Two equal ratios have cross products that are equal. This can be written as $\frac{m}{b} = \frac{w}{z}$. For example, Fred travels 2 miles in 1 hour, and Jane travels 4 miles in 2 hours. So, their speeds are proportional because $\frac{2}{1} = \frac{4}{2}$.

In a proportion, the product of the numerator of the first ratio and the denominator of the second ratio is equal to the product of the denominator of the first ratio and the numerator of the second ratio. In other words, you can see that $m \times z = b \times w$. So, $2 \times 2 = 1 \times 4$.

> **Review Video: Proportions**
> Visit mometrix.com/academy and enter code: 505355

ACTUAL DRAWINGS AND SCALE DRAWINGS

A map has a key for measurements to compare real distances with a scale distance.

Example: The key on one map says that 2 inches on the map is 12 real miles. Find the distance of a route that is 5 inches long on the map.

A proportion is needed to show the map measurements and real distances. First, write a ratio that has the information in the key. The map measurement can be in the numerator, and the real distance can be in the denominator.

$$\frac{2 \text{ inches}}{12 \text{ miles}}$$

Next, write a ratio with the known map distance and the unknown real distance. The unknown number for miles can be represented with the letter m.

$$\frac{5 \text{ inches}}{m \text{ miles}}$$

Then, write out the ratios in a proportion and solve it for m.

$$\frac{2 \text{ inches}}{12 \text{ miles}} = \frac{5 \text{ inches}}{m \text{ miles}}$$

Now, you have $2m = 60$. So you are left with $m = 30$. Thus, the route is 30 miles long.

Algebra, Functions, and Patterns

TRANSLATING
WORDS TO MATHEMATICAL EXPRESSION

Write "four less than twice x" as a mathematical expression.
Remember that an expression does not have an equal sign. "Less" indicates subtraction, and "twice" indicates multiplication by two. Four less than $2x$ is $2x - 4$. Notice how this is different than $4 - 2x$. You can plug in values for x to see how these expressions would yield different values.

WORDS TO MATHEMATICAL EQUATION

Translate "three hundred twenty-five increased by six times $3x$ equals three hundred forty-three" into a mathematical equation.
The key words and phrases are "increased by," "times," and "equals."
Three hundred twenty-five increased by six times $3x$ equals three hundred forty-three:
$$325 + 6(3x) = 343$$
The mathematical sentence is $325 + 6(3x) = 343$.

MATHEMATICAL EXPRESSION TO A PHRASE

Write a phrase which represents this mathematical expression: $75 - 3t + 14^2$.
Because there are many words which indicate various operations, there are several ways to write this expression, including "seventy-five minus three times t plus fourteen squared."

SOLVING FOR A VARIABLE

Similar to order of operation rules, algebraic rules must be obeyed to ensure a correct answer. Begin by locating all parentheses and brackets, and then solving the equations within them. Then, perform the operations necessary to remove all parentheses and brackets. Next, convert all fractions into whole numbers and combine common terms on each side of the equation.

Beginning on the left side of the expression, solve operations involving multiplication and division. Then, work left to right solving operations involving addition and subtraction. Finally, cross-multiply if necessary, to reach the final solution.

Example 1

$4a-10=10$

Constants are the numbers in equations that do not change. The variable in this equation is a. Variables are most commonly presented as either x or y, but they can be any letter. Every variable is equal to a number; one must solve the equation to determine what that number is. In an algebraic expression, the answer will usually be the number represented by the variable. In order to solve this equation, keep in mind that what is done to one side must be done to the other side as well. The first step will be to remove 10 from the left side by adding 10 to both sides. This will be expressed as $4a-10+10=10+10$, which simplifies to $4a=20$. Next, remove the 4 by dividing both sides by 4. This step will be expressed as $4a÷4=20÷4$. The expression now becomes $a=5$.

Since variables are the letters that represent an unknown number, you must solve for that unknown number in single variable problems. The main thing to remember is that you can do anything to one side of an equation as long as you do it to the other.

Example 2

Solve for x in the equation 2x + 3 = 5.

Answer: First you want to get the "2x" isolated by itself on one side. To do that, first get rid of the 3. Subtract 3 from both sides of the equation 2x + 3 – 3 = 5 – 3 or 2x = 2. Now since the x is being multiplied by the 2 in "2x", you must divide by 2 to get rid of it. So, divide both sides by 2, which gives 2x / 2 = 2 / 2 or x = 1.

MANIPULATING EQUATIONS

Sometimes you will have variables missing in equations. So, you need to find the missing variable. To do this, you need to remember one important thing: whatever you do to one side of an equation, you need to do to the other side. If you subtract 100 from one side of an equation, you need to subtract 100 from the other side of the equation. This will allow you to change the form of the equation to find missing values.

Example

Ray earns $10 an hour. This can be given with the expression $10x$, where x is equal to the number of hours that Ray works. This is the independent variable. The independent variable is the amount that can change. The money that Ray earns is in y hours. So, you would write the equation: $10x = y$. The variable y is the dependent variable. This depends on x and cannot be changed. Now, let's say that Ray makes $360. How many hours did he work to make $360?

$$10x = 360$$

Now, you want to know how many hours that Ray worked. So, you want to get x by itself. To do that, you can divide both sides of the equation by 10.

$$\frac{10x}{10} = \frac{360}{10}$$

So, you have: $x = 36$. Now, you know that Ray worked 36 hours to make $360.

FUNCTIONS

Example 1

The table below is the value of each part of an ordered pair. An ordered pair is written as: (x, y)

x	y
2	6
4	12
6	18
8	24

You can find y if you know x. The number in the y column is three times the number in the x column. Multiply the x number by 3 to get the y number.

x	y
2	$2 \times 3 = 6$
4	$4 \times 3 = 12$
6	$6 \times 3 = 18$
8	$8 \times 3 = 24$

Example 2

The table shows some data points for a linear function. What is the missing value in the table?

x	y
0	?
3	50
5	80

The data in the table represent a linear function. For a linear function, the rate of change is equal to the slope. To find the slope, calculate the change in y divided by the change in x for the two given points from the table: $m = \frac{80-50}{5-3} = \frac{30}{2} = 15$

The rate of change of the linear function is 15. This means for each increase of 1 in the value of x, the value of y increases by 15. Similarly, each decrease of 1 in the value of x decreases the value of y by 15. The x-value 0 is 3 less than 3, so subtract $3 \cdot 15 = 45$ from 50 to get y = 5. This is the missing value in the table.

SEQUENCING

Example 1

Use the sequence to find each of the following.

6, 13, 20, 27, 34, 41, ...

a) Find the position of 34.

b) Find the value of the term in position 7.

a) The position of a term is its place in the sequence. The sequence begins with 6, in position 1, 13 is position 2, etc. The term 34 has a position of 5.

b) The terms in positions 1 through 6 are given. To find the term in position 7, identify the difference between each term.

13 – 6 = 7

20 – 13 = 7

27 – 20 = 7

34 – 27 = 7

41 – 34 = 7

The terms are increasing by 7. To find the 7th term, add 7 to the sixth term, 41:

41 + 7 = 48

The term in position 7 is 48.

Example 2

The *n*th term of a sequence is: 4*n* – 6. Find the terms in position: 1, 4, and 10.

To find the terms in each given position, evaluate the expression for the *n*th term at the given position values.

1st term: 4(1) – 6 = 4 – 6 = –2

4th term: 4(4) – 6 = 16 – 6 = 10

10th term: 4(10) – 6 = 40 – 6 = 34

Example 3

Write an algebraic expression to determine the *n*th term of the arithmetic sequence:

31, 25, 19, 13, ...

To find the *n*th term, find the common difference between each pair of given terms.

2nd term – 1st term: 25 – 31 = –6

3rd term – 2nd term: 19 – 25 = –6

4th term – 3rd term: 13 – 19 = –6

The first term is 31, so when *n* = 1, the term is 31.

1st term: 31 + –6(*n* – 1)

Simplify this expression and check it for terms 2, 3, and 4 by evaluating the expression at n = 2, 3, and 4.

$31 + -6(n - 1) = 31 - 6n + 6 = -6n + 37$

2nd term: $-6(2) + 37 = -12 + 37 = 25$

3rd term: $-6(3) + 37 = -18 + 37 = 19$

4th term: $-6(4) + 37 = -24 + 37 = 13$

The nth term of the arithmetic sequence is $-6n + 37$.

Geometry

LINES AND PLANES

A point is a fixed location in space. This point has no size or dimensions. Commonly, this fixed location is a dot. A collinear point is a point which is on the line. A non-collinear point is a point that is not on a line.

A line is a set of points that go forever in two opposite directions. The line has length but no width or depth. A line can be named by any two points that are on the line. A line segment is a part of a line that has definite endpoints. A ray is a part of a line that goes from a single point and goes in one direction along the line. A ray has a definite beginning but no ending.

A plane is a two-dimensional flat surface that has three non-collinear points. A plane goes an unending distance in all directions in those two dimensions. This plane has an unending number of points, parallel lines and segments, intersecting lines and segments. Also, a plane can have an unending number of parallel or intersecting rays. A plane will never have a three-dimensional figure or skew lines. Two given planes will be parallel, or they will intersect to form a line. A plane may intersect a circular conic surface (e.g., a cone) to make conic sections (e.g., the parabola, hyperbola, circle, or ellipse).

Perpendicular lines are lines that intersect at right angles. The symbol ⊥ stands for perpendicular lines. The shortest distance from a line to a point that is not on the line is a perpendicular segment from the point to the line.

Parallel lines are lines in the same plane that have no points in common and never meet. The lines can be in different planes, have no points in common, and never meet. However, the lines will not be parallel because they are in different planes.

A bisector is a line or line segment that divides another line segment into two equal lengths. A perpendicular bisector of a line segment has points that are equidistant (i.e., equal distances) from the endpoints of the segment.

Intersecting lines are lines that have exactly one point in common. Concurrent lines are several lines that intersect at a single point. A transversal is a line that intersects at least two other lines. The lines may or may not be parallel to one another. A transversal that intersects parallel lines is common in geometry.

COORDINATE PLANE

Often, algebraic functions and equations are shown on a graph. This graph is known as the *Cartesian Coordinate Plane*. The Cartesian coordinate plane has two number lines that are perpendicular. These lines intersect at the zero point. This point is also known as the origin. The horizontal number line is known as the *x*-axis.

On the *x*-axis, there are positive values to the right of the origin and negative values to the left of the origin. The vertical number line is known as the *y*-axis. There are positive values above the origin and negative values below the origin. Any point on the plane can be found with an ordered pair.

This ordered pair comes in the form of (x, y). This pair is known as coordinates. The *x*-value of the coordinate is called the abscissa. The *y*-value of the coordinate is called the ordinate. The two number lines divide the plane into four parts. Each part is known as a quadrant. The quadrants are labeled as I, II, III, and IV.

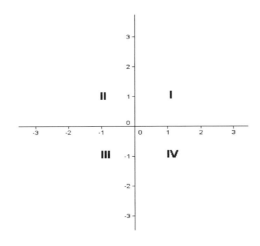

Example 1

The following points go on the coordinate plane:

A. $(-4, -2)$ | B. $(-1, 3)$ | C. $(2, 2)$ | D. $(3, -1)$

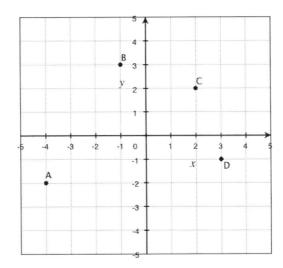

TRANSFORMATION

- Rotation: An object is rotated, or turned, between 0 and 360 degrees, around a fixed point. The size and shape of the object are unchanged.
- Reflection: An object is reflected, or flipped, across a line, so that the original object and reflected object are the same distance from the line of reflection. The size and shape of the object are unchanged.
- Translation: An object is translated, or shifted, horizontally and/or vertically to a new location. The orientation, size, and shape of the object are unchanged.

ROTATION

A line segment begins at (1, 4) and ends at (5, 4). Draw the line segment and rotate the line segment 90º about the point (3, 4).

The point about which the line segment is being rotated is on the line segment. This point should be on both the original and rotated line. The point (3, 4) is the center of the original line segment, and should still be the center of the rotated line segment. The dashed line is the rotated line segment.

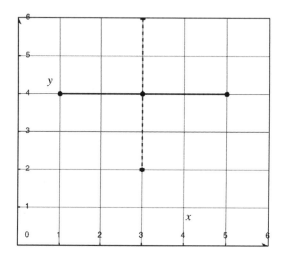

REFLECTION

Example 1: To create a congruent rectangle by reflecting, first draw a line of reflection. The line can be next to or on the figure. Then draw the image reflected across this line.

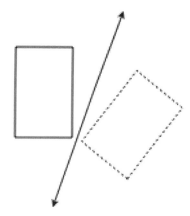

34

Example 2: A line segment begins at (1, 5) and ends at (5, 4). Draw the line segment, then reflect the line segment across the line *y* = 3.

To reflect a segment, consider folding a piece of paper at the line of reflection. The new image should line up exactly with the old image when the paper is folded. The dashed line is the reflected line segment.

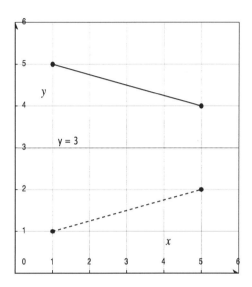

TRANSLATION

Example 1: A line segment on an x-y grid starts at (3, 2) and ends at (4, 1). Draw the line segment, and translate the segment up 2 units and left 2 units.

The solid line segment is the original line segment, and the dashed line is the translated line segment. The *y*-coordinate of each point has increased by 2, because the points moved two units away from 0. The *x*-coordinate of each point has decreased by 2, because the points moved two units closer to 0.

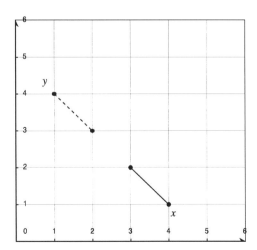

35

Example 2: Identify a transformation that could have been performed on the solid triangle to result in the dashed triangle.

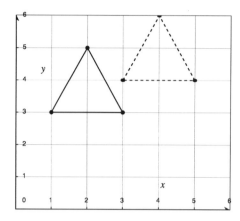

The transformed triangle has the same orientation as the original triangle. It has been shifted up one unit and two units to the right. Because the orientation of the figure has not changed, and its new position can be described using shifts up and to the right, the figure was translated.

ANGLES

An angle is made when two lines or line segments meet at a point. The angle may be a starting point for a pair of segments or rays. Also, angles come from the intersection of lines. The symbol ∠ stands for angles. Angles that are opposite to one another are called vertical angles, and their measures are equal. The vertex is the point where two segments or rays meet to make an angle. Angles that are made from intersecting rays, lines, and/or line segments have four angles at the vertex.

An acute angle is an angle with a degree measure less than 90°. A right angle is an angle with a degree measure of exactly 90°. An obtuse angle is an angle with a degree measure greater than 90° but less than 180°. A straight angle is an angle with a degree measure of exactly 180°. A reflex angle is an angle with a degree measure greater than 180° but less than 360°. A full angle is an angle with a degree measure of exactly 360°.

> **Review Video: Angles**
> Visit mometrix.com/academy and enter code: 264624

Two angles with a sum of exactly 90° are known as complementary. The two angles may or may not be adjacent (i.e., *next to* or *beside*). In a right triangle, the two acute angles are complementary.

Two angles with a sum that is exactly 180° are known as supplementary. The two angles may or may not be adjacent. Two intersecting lines always make two pairs of supplementary angles. Adjacent supplementary angles will always make a straight line.

TRIANGLES

An equilateral triangle is a triangle with three congruent sides. Also, an equilateral triangle will have three congruent angles and each angle will be 60°. All equilateral triangles are acute triangles.

36

An isosceles triangle is a triangle with two congruent sides. An isosceles triangle will have two congruent angles as well.

A scalene triangle is a triangle with no congruent sides. Also, a scalene triangle will have three angles of different measures. The angle with the largest measure is opposite from the longest side. The angle with the smallest measure is opposite from the shortest side.

An acute triangle is a triangle whose three angles are all less than 90°. If two of the angles are equal, the acute triangle is also an isosceles triangle. If the three angles are all equal, the acute triangle is also an equilateral triangle.

A right triangle is a triangle with exactly one angle equal to 90°. A right triangle can never be acute or obtuse.

An obtuse triangle is a triangle with one angle greater than 90°. The other two angles may or may not be equal. If the two remaining angles are equal, the obtuse triangle is also an isosceles triangle.

CONGRUENCY, SIMILARITY, AND SYMMETRY

Congruent figures are geometric figures that have the same size and shape. All corresponding angles are equal, and all corresponding sides are equal. Congruence is shown by the symbol ≅.

Congruent polygons

Similar figures are geometric figures that have the same shape, but may not have the same size. All corresponding angles are equal, and all corresponding sides are proportional. However, they do not have to be equal. Similarity is shown by the symbol ~.

Similar polygons

Note that all congruent figures are also similar. However, not all similar figures are congruent.

Line of Symmetry: The line that divides a figure or object into equal parts. Each part is congruent to the other. An object may have no lines of symmetry, one line of symmetry, or multiple (i.e., more than one) lines of symmetry.

Lines of symmetry:

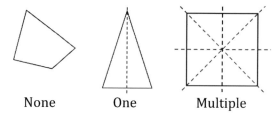

None   One   Multiple

POLYGONS AND TWO-DIMENSIONAL FIGURES

Each straight line segment of a polygon is called a side. The point at which two sides of a polygon intersect is called the vertex. In a polygon, the number of sides is always equal to the number of vertices. A polygon with all sides congruent and all angles equal is called a regular polygon.

A line segment from the center of a polygon that is perpendicular to a side of the polygon is called the apothem. A line segment from the center of a polygon to a vertex of the polygon is called a radius. In a regular polygon, the apothem can be used to find the area of the polygon using the formula $A = \frac{1}{2}ap$, where a is the apothem, and p is the perimeter.

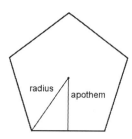

- Triangle – 3 sides
- Quadrilateral – 4 sides
- Pentagon – 5 sides
- Hexagon – 6 sides
- Heptagon – 7 sides
- Octagon – 8 sides
- Nonagon – 9 sides
- Decagon – 10 sides
- Dodecagon – 12 sides

Generally, an n-gon is a polygon that has more than 12 angles and sides. The space of n is for the number of sides. Also, an 11-sided polygon is known as an 11-gon.

Quadrilateral: A closed two-dimensional geometric figure that has four straight sides. The sum of the interior angles of any quadrilateral is 360°. A quadrilateral whose diagonals divide each other is a parallelogram.

A quadrilateral whose opposite sides are parallel (i.e., 2 pairs of parallel sides) is a parallelogram. A quadrilateral whose diagonals are perpendicular bisectors of each other is a rhombus. A quadrilateral with opposite sides (i.e., both pairs) that are parallel and congruent is a rhombus.

Parallelogram: A quadrilateral that has two pairs of opposite parallel sides. The sides that are parallel are also congruent. The opposite interior angles are always congruent, and the consecutive interior angles are supplementary. The diagonals of a parallelogram divide each other. Each diagonal divides the parallelogram into two congruent triangles.

A parallelogram that has a right angle is a rectangle. In the diagram below, the top left corner and the bottom left corner are consecutive angles. Consecutive angles of a parallelogram are supplementary. If there is one right angle in a parallelogram, there are four right angles in that parallelogram.

Trapezoid: Normally, a quadrilateral has one pair of parallel sides. Some define a trapezoid as a quadrilateral that has at least one pair of parallel sides. There are no rules for the second pair of sides. So, there are no rules for the diagonals of a trapezoid.

Rectangles, rhombuses, and squares are all special forms of parallelograms.

Rectangle: A parallelogram with four right angles. All rectangles are parallelograms, but not all parallelograms are rectangles. The diagonals of a rectangle are congruent.

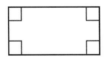

Rhombus: A parallelogram with four congruent sides. All rhombuses are parallelograms, but not all parallelograms are rhombuses. The diagonals of a rhombus are perpendicular to each other.

A rhombus with one right angle is a square. The rhombus is a special form of a parallelogram. So, the rules about the angles of a parallelogram are true for the rhombus.

Square: A parallelogram with four right angles and four congruent sides. All squares are also parallelograms, rhombuses, and rectangles. The diagonals of a square are congruent and perpendicular to each other.

THREE DIMENSIONAL FIGURES

RIGHT RECTANGULAR PRISM

A rectangular prism has six rectangular faces. The six faces give it 12 edges and eight vertices.

CUBE

A cube has six square faces. The six faces give it 12 edges and eight vertices.

40

SPHERE

A sphere is a perfectly round object that has no faces, edges, or vertices. This three-dimensional object is similar to the two-dimensional circle.

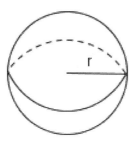

RIGHT TRIANGULAR PRISM

A triangular prism has five faces. Two faces are triangles, and three faces are rectangles. This prism has 9 edges and six vertices.

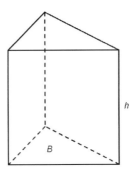

CYLINDER

The cylinder has two circular faces. In three dimensions, the cylinder has edges or vertices.

RIGHT RECTANGULAR PYRAMID

A rectangular pyramid has four triangular faces and one rectangular face. This pyramid has eight edges and five vertices.

CONE

A cone has one circular face. Cones do not have any edges or vertices. The cones that you will encounter are right circular. This means that they have a circle for a base instead of a polygonal base. A pyramid is a cone with a polygonal base.

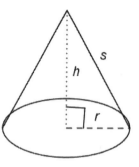

Measurement

AREA AND PERIMETER FORMULAS

The perimeter of any triangle is found by adding the three side lengths $P = a + b + c$. For an equilateral triangle, this is the same as $P = 3s$, where s is any side length. The reason is that the three sides are the same length.

The area of any triangle can be found by taking half of the base (i.e., b). Then, multiply that result by the height (i.e., h) of the triangle. So, the standard formula for the area of a triangle is $A = \frac{1}{2}bh$. For many triangles, it may be difficult to calculate h. So, other formulas are given here that may be easier.

Note: When you need to find the height, you can follow the steps above to find it.

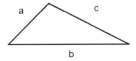

Another formula that works for any triangle is $A = \sqrt{s(s-a)(s-b)(s-c)}$, where A is the area, s is the semi-perimeter $s = \frac{a+b+c}{2}$, and a, b, and c are the lengths of the three sides. The area of an equilateral triangle can be found by the formula $A = \frac{\sqrt{3}}{4}s^2$, where A is the area and s is the length of a side. You could use the $30° - 60° - 90°$ ratios to find the height of the triangle. Then, use the standard triangle area formula.

The area of an isosceles triangle can be found by the formula, $A = \frac{1}{2}b\sqrt{a^2 - \frac{b^2}{4}}$, where A is the area, b is the base, and a is the length of one of the two congruent sides. If you do not remember this formula, you can use the Pythagorean Theorem to find the height. Then, you can use the standard formula for the area of a triangle.

The area of a square is found by using the formula $A = s^2$, where A is the area and s is the length of one side.

The perimeter of a square is found by using the formula $P = 4s$, where P is the perimeter, and s is the length of one side. All four sides are equal in a square. So, you can multiply the length of one side by 4. This is faster than adding the same number four times.

The area of a rectangle is found by the formula $A = lw$, where A is the area of the rectangle, l is the length and w is the width. Usually, the longer side is the length, and the shorter side is the width. However, the numbers for l and w can used be for one or the other.

The perimeter of a rectangle can be found with two formulas $P = 2l + 2w$ or $P = 2(l + w)$, where l is the length, and w is the width.

The area of a parallelogram is found by the formula $A = bh$, where b is the length of the base, and h is the height. Note that the base and height match with the length and width in a rectangle. So, this formula can be used for rectangles as well. Do not confuse the height of a parallelogram with the length of the second side. They have the same measure only with rectangles.

The perimeter of a parallelogram is found by the formula $P = 2a + 2b$ or $P = 2(a + b)$, where a and b are the lengths of the two sides.

The area of a trapezoid is found by the formula $A = \frac{1}{2}h(b_1 + b_2)$, where h is the height, and b_1 and b_2 are the two parallel sides (i.e., bases). The height is the segment that joins the parallel bases.

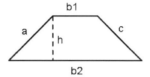

The perimeter of a trapezoid is found by the formula $P = a + b_1 + c + b_2$, where a, b_1, c, and b_2 are the four sides of the trapezoid.

CIRCLES

The center is the single point inside the circle that is equidistant from every point on the circle. The point O is in the diagram below. The radius is a line segment that joins the center of the circle and any one point on the circle. All radii of a circle are equal. The segments OX, OY, and OZ are in the diagram below. The diameter is a line segment that passes through the center of the circle and has both endpoints inside the circle. The length of the diameter is twice the length of the radius. The segment XZ is in the diagram below. Concentric circles are circles that have the same center but not the same length of radii. A bulls-eye target is an example of concentric circles.

The **area of a circle** is found with the formula $A = \pi r^2$, where r is the length of the radius. If the diameter of the circle is given, divide it in half to get the radius before using the formula. (Note: In the following formulas, 3.14 is used for π.)

The **circumference of a circle** is found by the formula $C = 2\pi r$, where r is the radius.

SURFACE AREA AND VOLUME FORMULAS
RECTANGULAR PRISM

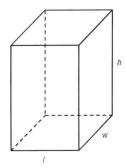

The **volume of a rectangular prism** can be found with the formula $V = lwh$, where V is the volume, l is the length, w is the width, and h is the height.

The **surface area of a rectangular prism** can be calculated as $SA = 2lw + 2hl + 2wh$ or $SA = 2(lw + hl + wh)$.

CUBE

The **volume of a cube** can be found with the formula $V = s^3$, where s is the length of a side.

The **surface area of a cube** is calculated as $SA = 6s^2$, where SA is the total surface area and s is the length of a side. These formulas are the same as the ones used for the volume and surface area of a rectangular prism. However, these are simple formulas because the three numbers (i.e., length, width, and height) are the same.

TEMPERATURE

Find the temperature, in degrees Fahrenheit, on the thermometer below. Use the thermometer to find the temperature if the temperature increased by 5° Fahrenheit.

45

The temperature, on the thermometer, is 75° F. If the temperature increases by 5° F, change the thermometer to show the increase in 5°:

If the temperature increases by 5° F, the new temperature is 80° F.

TIME

Lindsay leaves for school at 7:00am. It takes her 20 minutes to get to school. Use a clock to determine the time Lindsay arrives at school. 7:00 am means the large clock hand is on 12, and the small hand is on 7.

In 20 minutes, the big hand will move 20 minutes clockwise, to the 4. The big hand will also move closer to the 8. 20 minutes is: $\frac{20}{60} = \frac{1}{3}$ of an hour, so the big hand will move one third of the way from the 7 to the 8.

The ending time is 7:20am, which is when Lindsay arrives at school.

Data Analysis and Probability

MEASURES OF CENTRAL TENDENCY

The quantities of mean, median, and mode are known as measures of central tendency. Each can give a picture of what a whole set of data looks like with a single number. Knowing what each value stands for is important to understanding the information from these measures.

MEAN

The mean, or the arithmetic mean or average, of a data set is found by adding all of the values in the set. Then you divide the sum by how many values that you had in a set. For example, a data set has 6 numbers, and the sum of those 6 numbers is 30. So, the mean is 30/6 = 5. When you know the average, you may be asked to find a missing value. Look over the following steps for how this is done.

Example: You are given the values of 5, 10, 12, and 13. Also, you are told that the average is 9.6. So, what is the one missing value?

First: Add the known values together: $5 + 10 + 12 + 13 = 40$.

Now, set up an equation with the sum of the known values in the divisor. Then, put the number of values in the dividend.

For this example, you have 5 values. So, you have $\frac{40+?}{5} = 9.6$. Now, multiply both sides by 5: $5 \times \frac{40+?}{5} = 9.6 \times 5$

Second: You are left with $40 + ? = 48$. Now, subtract 40 from both sides: $40 - 40 + ? = 48 - 40$. So, you know that the missing value is 8.

MEDIAN

The median is the middle value of a data set. The median can be found by putting the data set in numerical order (e.g., 3, 7, 26, 28, 39). Then, you pick the value that is in the middle of the set. In the data set (1, 2, 3, 4, 5), there is an odd number of values. So, the median is 3. Sometimes, there is an even number of values in the set. So, the median can be found by taking the average of the two middle values. In the data set (1, 2, 3, 4, 5, 6), the median would be (3 + 4)/2 = 3.5.

MODE

The mode is the value that appears the most in a data set. In the data set (1, 2, 3, 4, 5, 5, 5), the number 5 appears more than the other numbers. So, the value 5 is the mode. If more than one value appears the same number of times, then there are multiple values for the mode. For example, a data set is (1, 2, 2, 3, 4, 4, 5, 5). So, the modes would be 2, 4, and 5. Now, if no value appears more than any other value in the data set, then there is no mode.

> **Review Video: Mean, Median, and Mode**
> Visit mometrix.com/academy and enter code: 286207

RANGE

The range is the difference between the greatest data point and the least data point in the set. In the set (12, 23, 1, 8, 45, 22), the greatest data point is 45. The least data point is 1. When you subtract 1 from 45, you have 44. So, 44 is the range of the data set.

COMMON CHARTS AND GRAPHS

Charts and *Tables* are ways of organizing information into separate rows and columns. These rows and columns are labeled to find and to explain the information in them. Some charts and tables are organized horizontally with rows giving the details about the labeled information. Other charts and tables are organized vertically with columns giving the details about the labeled information.

A *Bar Graph* is one of the few graphs that can be drawn correctly in two ways: horizontally and vertically. A bar graph is similar to a line plot because of how the data is organized on the graph. Both axes must have their categories defined for the graph to be useful. A thick line is drawn from zero to the exact value of the data. This line can be used for a number, a percentage, or other numerical value. Longer bar lengths point to greater data values. To understand a bar graph, read the labels for the axes to know the units being reported. Then look where the bars end and match this to the scale on the other axis. This will show you the connection between the axes. This bar graph shows the responses from a survey about the favorite colors of a group.

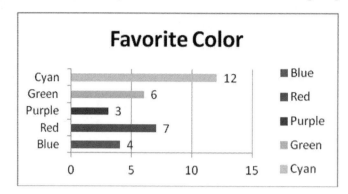

Line Graphs have one or more lines of different styles (e.g., solid or broken). These lines show the different values for a data set. Each point on the graph is shown as an ordered pair. This is similar to a Cartesian plane. In this case, the *x*- and *y*- axes are given certain units (e.g., dollars or time). Each point that is for one measurement is joined by line segments. Then, these lines show what the values are doing. The lines may be increasing (i.e., line sloping upward), decreasing (i.e., line sloping downward), or staying the same (i.e., horizontal line). More than one set of data can be put on the same line graph. This is done to compare more than one piece of data. An example of this would be graphing test scores for different groups of students over the same stretch of time. This allows you to see which group had the greatest increase or decrease in performance over a certain amount of years. This example is shown in the graph below.

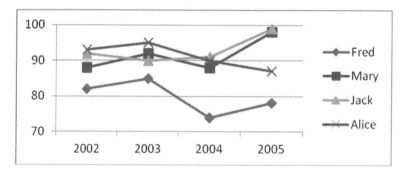

A *Line Plot*, or a *Dot Plot*, has plotted points that are NOT connected by line segments. In this graph, the horizontal axis lists the different possible values for the data. The vertical axis lists how many times one value happens. A single dot is graphed for each value. The dots in a line plot are connected. If the dots are connected, then this will not correctly represent the data.

A *Pictograph* is a graph that is given in the horizontal format. This graph uses pictures or symbols to show the data. Each pictograph must have a key that defines the picture or symbol. Also, this key should give the number that stands for each picture or symbol. The pictures or symbols on a pictograph are not always shown as whole elements.

In this case, the fraction of the picture or symbol stands for the same fraction of the quantity that a whole picture or symbol represents. For example, there is a row in the pictograph with $3\frac{1}{2}$ ears of corn. Each ear of corn represents 100 stalks of corn in a field. So, this would equal $3\frac{1}{2} \times 100 = 350$ stalks of corn in the field.

Circle Graphs, or *Pie Charts*, show the relationship of each type of data compared to the whole set of data. The circle graph is divided into sections by drawing radii (i.e., plural for radius) to make central angles. These angles stand for a percentage of the circle. Each 1% of data is equal to 3.6° in the graph. So, data that stands for a 90° section of the circle graph makes up 25% of the whole. The pie chart below shows the data from the frequency table where people were asked about their favorite color.

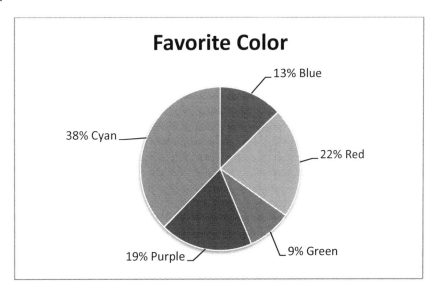

PROBABILITY

Probability is a branch of statistics that deals with the likelihood of something taking place. One classic example is a coin toss. There are only two possible results: heads or tails. The likelihood, or probability, that the coin will land as heads is 1 out of 2 (i.e., 1/2, 0.5, 50%). Tails has the same probability. Another common example is a 6-sided die roll. There are six possible results from rolling a single die. So, each side has an equal chance of happening. So, the probability of any number coming up is 1 out of 6.

> **Review Video: <u>Intro to Probability</u>**
> Visit mometrix.com/academy and enter code: 212374

Reading Comprehension

Reading and Thinking

ORGANIZATION OF THE PASSAGE

The way a passage is organized can help readers to understand the author's purpose and his or her conclusions. There are many ways to organize a passage, and each one has an important use.

Sometimes authors will organize information clearly for you to follow and locate the information. However, this is not always the case with passages in an exam. Two common ways to order a passage are cause and effect and chronological order. When using **chronological order** (i.e., a plan that moves in order from the first step to the last), the author gives information in the order that the event happened. For example, biographies are written in chronological order. The person's birth and childhood are first. Their adult life is next. The events leading up to the person's death are last.

PURPOSES FOR WRITING

An **informative passage** is written to teach readers. Informative passages are almost always nonfiction. The purpose of an informative passage is to share information in the clearest way. In an informative passage, you may have a thesis statement (i.e., an argument on the topic of a passage that is explained by proof). A thesis statement is a sentence that normally comes at end of the first paragraph. Authors of informative passages are likely to put more importance on being clear. Informative passages do not normally appeal to the feelings. They often contain facts and figures. Informative passages almost never include the opinion of the author. However, you should know that there can be a bias in the facts. Sometimes, a persuasive passage can be like an informative passage. This is true when authors give their ideas as if they were facts.

Entertainment passages describe real or imagined people, places, and events. Entertainment passages are often stories or poems. So, figurative language is a common part of these passages. Often, an entertainment passage appeals to the imagination and feelings. Authors may persuade or inform in an entertainment passage. Or, an entertainment passage may cause readers to think differently about a subject.

When authors want to **share feelings,** they may use strong language. Authors may share feelings about a moment of great pain or happiness. Other times, authors will try to persuade readers by sharing feelings. Some phrases like *I felt* and *I sense* hint that the author is sharing feelings. Authors may share a story of deep pain or great joy. You must not be influenced by these stories. You need to keep some distance to judge the author's argument.

Almost all writing is descriptive. In one way or another, authors try to describe events, ideas, or people. Some texts are concerned only with **description**. A descriptive passage focuses on a single subject and seeks to explain the subject clearly. Descriptive passages contain many adjectives and adverbs (i.e., words that give a complete picture for you to imagine). Normally, a descriptive passage is informative. Yet, the passage may be persuasive or entertaining.

WRITING DEVICES

Authors will use different writing devices to make their message clear for readers. One of those devices is comparison and contrast. When authors show how two things are alike, they are **comparing** them. When authors describe how two things are different, they are **contrasting** them.

50

The compare and contrast passage is a common part of nonfiction. Comparisons are known by certain words or phrases: *both*, *same*, *like*, *too*, and *as well*. Yet, contrasts may have words or phrases like *but*, *however*, *on the other hand*, *instead*, and *yet*. Of course, comparisons and contrasts may be understood without using those words or phrases. A single sentence may compare and contrast. Think about the sentence *Brian and Sheila love ice cream, but Brian loves vanilla and Sheila loves strawberry*. In one sentence, the author has described both a similarity (e.g., love of ice cream) and a difference (e.g., favorite flavor).

> **Review Video: Compare and Contrast Essays**
> Visit mometrix.com/academy and enter code: 798319

Point of view has an important influence on a passage. A passage's point of view is how the author or a character sees or thinks about things. A point of view influences the events of a passage, the meetings among characters, and the ending to the story. For example, two characters watch a child ride a bike. Character one watches outside. Character two watches from inside a house. Both see the same event, yet they are around different noises, sights, and smells. Character one may see different things that happen outside that character two cannot see from inside. Also, point of view can be influenced by past events and beliefs. For example, if character one loves bikes, then she will remember how proud she is of the child. If character two is afraid of riding bikes, then he may not remember the event or fear for the child's safety.

In fiction, the two main points of view are first person and third person. The narrator is the person who tells a story's events. The protagonist is the main character of a story. If the narrator is the protagonist in a story, then the story is written in first-person. In first person, the author writes from the view of *I*. Third-person point of view is the most common among stories. With third person, authors refer to each character by using *he* or *she* and the narrator is not involved in the story. In third-person omniscient, the narrator is not a character in the story and tells the story of all of the characters at the same time.

> **Review Video: Point of View**
> Visit mometrix.com/academy and enter code: 383336

Transitional words and phrases are devices that guide readers through a passage. You may know the common transitions. Though you may not have thought about how they are used. Some transitional phrases (*after*, *before*, *during*, *in the middle of*) give information about time. Some hint that an example is about to be given (*for example*, *in fact*, *for instance*). Writers use transitions to compare (*also*, *likewise*) and contrast (*however*, *but*, *yet*). Transitional words and phrases can point to addition (*and*, *also*, *furthermore*, *moreover*) and understood relationships (*if*, *then*, *therefore*, *as a result*, *since*). Finally, transitional words and phrases can separate the chronological steps (*first*, *second*, *last*).

> **Review Video: Transitional Words and Phrases**
> Visit mometrix.com/academy and enter code: 197796

UNDERSTANDING A PASSAGE

One of the most important skills in reading comprehension is finding **topics** and **main ideas.** There is a small difference between these two. The topic is the subject of a passage (i.e., what the passage is all about). The main idea is the most important argument being made by the author. The topic is shared in a few words while the main idea needs a full sentence to be understood. As an example, a short passage might have the topic of penguins, and the main idea could be written as *Penguins are different from other birds in many ways.*

In most nonfiction writing, the topic and the main idea will be stated clearly. Sometimes, they will come in a sentence at the very beginning or end of the passage. When you want to know the topic, you may find it in the first sentence of each paragraph. A body paragraph's first sentence is often--but not always--the main topic sentence. The topic sentence gives you a summary of the ideas in the paragraph. You may find that the topic or main idea is not given clearly. So, you must read every sentence of the passage. Then, try to come up with an overall idea from each sentence.

Note: A thesis statement is not the same as the main idea. The main idea gives a brief, general summary of a text. The thesis statement gives a clear idea on an issue that is backed up with evidence.

> **Review Video: Topics and Main Ideas**
> Visit mometrix.com/academy and enter code: 407801

The main idea is the umbrella argument of a passage. So, **supporting details** back up the main idea. To show that a main idea is correct, authors add details that prove their idea. All passages contain details. However, they are referred to as supporting details when they help an argument in the passage. Supporting details are found in informative and persuasive texts. Sometimes they will come with terms like *for example* or *for instance*. Or, they will be numbered with terms like *first*, *second*, and *last*. You should think about how the author's supporting details back up his or her main idea. Supporting details can be correct, yet they may help the author's main idea. Sometimes supporting details can seem helpful. However, they may be useless when they are based on opinions.

> **Review Video: Supporting Details**
> Visit mometrix.com/academy and enter code: 396297

An example of a main idea: *Giraffes live in the Serengeti of Africa.* A supporting detail about giraffes could be: *A giraffe in the Serengeti benefits from a long neck by reaching twigs and leaves on tall trees.* The main idea gives the general idea that the text is about giraffes. The supporting detail gives a clear fact about how the giraffes eat.

A **theme** is an issue, an idea, or a question raised by a passage. For example, a theme of *Cinderella* is determination as Cinderella serves her step-sisters and step-mother. Passages may have many themes, and you must be sure to find only themes that you are asked to find. One common mark of themes is that they give more questions than answers. Authors try to push readers to consider themes in other ways. You can find themes by asking about the general problems that the passage is addressing. A good way to find a theme is to begin reading with a question in mind (e.g., How does this passage use the theme of love?) and to look for answers to that question.

> **Review Video: Theme**
> Visit mometrix.com/academy and enter code: 732074

EVALUATING A PASSAGE

When you read informational passages, you need to make a conclusion from the author's writing. You can **identify a logical conclusion** (i.e., find a conclusion that makes sense) to know whether you agree or disagree with an author. Coming to this conclusion is like making an inference. You combine the information from the passage with what you already know. From the passage's

52

information and your knowledge, you can come to a conclusion that makes sense. One way to have a conclusion that makes sense is to take notes of all the author's points. When the notes are organized, they may point to the logical conclusion. Another way to reach conclusions is to ask if the author's passage raises any helpful questions. Sometimes you will be able to draw many conclusions from a passage. Yet, some of these may be conclusions that were never imagined by the author. Therefore, find reasons in the passage for the conclusions that you make.

> **Review Video: <u>Identifying Logical Conclusions</u>**
> Visit mometrix.com/academy and enter code: 281653

Text evidence is the information that supports a main argument or minor argument. This evidence, or proof, can lead you to a conclusion. Information used as text evidence is clear, descriptive, and full of facts. Supporting details give evidence to back-up an argument.

For example, a passage may state that winter occurs during opposite months in the Northern hemisphere (i.e., north of the equator) and Southern hemisphere (i.e., south of the equator). Text evidence for this claim may include a list of countries where winter occurs in opposite months. Also, you may be given reasons that winter occurs at different times of the year in these hemispheres (e.g., the tilt of the Earth as it rotates around the sun).

> **Review Video: <u>Text Evidence</u>**
> Visit mometrix.com/academy and enter code: 486236

A reader should always draw conclusions from passages. Sometimes conclusions are implied (i.e., information that is assumed) from written information. Other times the information is **stated directly** within the passage. You should try to draw conclusions from information stated in a passage. Furthermore, you should always read through the entire passage before drawing conclusions. Many readers expect the author's conclusions at the beginning or the end of the passage. However, many texts do not follow this format.

Implications are things that the author does not say directly. Yet, you can assume from what the author does say. For example, *I stepped outside and opened my umbrella. By the time I got to work, the cuffs of my pants were soaked.* The author never says that it is raining. However, you can conclude that this information is implied. Conclusions from implications must be well supported by the passage. To draw a conclusion, you should have many pieces of proof. Yet, let's say that you have only one piece. Then, you need to be sure that there is no other possible explanation than your conclusion. Practice drawing conclusions from implications in real life events to improve your skills.

Outlining the information in a passage should be a well-known skill to readers. A good outline will show the pattern of the passage and lead to better conclusions. A common outline calls for the main ideas of the passage to be listed in the order that they come. Then, beneath each main idea, you can list the minor ideas and details. An outline does not need to include every detail from the passage. However, the outline should show everything that is important to the argument.

Another helpful tool is the skill of **summarizing** information. This process is similar to creating an outline. First, a summary should define the main idea of the passage. The summary should have the most important supporting details or arguments. Summaries can be unclear or wrong because they do not stay true to the information in the passage. A helpful summary should have the same message as the passage.

Ideas from a passage can be organized using **graphic organizers**. A graphic organizer reduces information to a few key points. A graphic organizer like a timeline may have an event listed for each date on the timeline. However, an outline may have an event listed under a key point that happens in the passage.

Review Video: Graphic Organizers
Visit mometrix.com/academy and enter code: 665513

You need to make a graphic organizer that works best for you. Whatever helps you remember information from a passage is what you need to use. A spider-map is another example. This map takes a main idea from the story and places it in a bubble. From one main idea bubble, you put supporting points that connect to the main idea. A Venn diagram groups information as separate or connected with some overlap.

Paraphrasing is another method that you can use to understand a passage. To paraphrase, you put what you have read into your own words. Or, you can *translate* what the author shared into your words by including as many details as you can.

RESPONDING TO A PASSAGE

One part of being a good reader is making predictions. A **prediction** is a guess about what will happen next. Readers make predictions from what they have read and what they already know. For example: *Staring at the computer screen in shock, Kim reached for the glass of water.* The sentence leaves you to think that she is not looking at the glass. So, you may guess that Kim is going to knock over the glass. Yet, in the next sentence, you may read that Kim does not knock over the glass. As you have more information, be ready for your predictions to change.

Review Video: Predictions
Visit mometrix.com/academy and enter code: 437248

Test-taking tip: To respond to questions that ask about predictions, your answer should come from the passage.

You will be asked to understand text that gives ideas without stating them directly. An **inference** is something that is implied but not stated directly by the author. For example: *After the final out of the inning, the fans were filled with joy and rushed the field*. From this sentence, you can infer that the fans were watching baseball and their team won. You should not use information outside of the passage before making inferences. As you practice making inferences, you will find that they need all of your attention.

Review Video: Inference
Visit mometrix.com/academy and enter code: 379203

Test-taking tip: When asked about inferences, look for context clues. Context is what surrounds the words and sentences that add explanation or information to an unknown piece. An answer can be *true* but not *correct*. The context clues will help you find the answer that is best. When asked for the implied meaning of a statement, you should locate the statement first. Then, read the context around the statement. Finally, look for an answer with a similar phrase.

For your exam, you must be able to find a text's **sequence** (i.e., the order that things happen). When the sequence is very important to the author, the passage comes with signal words: *first, then, next,* and *last*. However, a sequence can be implied. For example, *He walked through the garden and gave* *water and fertilizer to the plants.* Clearly, the man did not walk through the garden at the beginning. First, he found water. Then, he collected fertilizer. Next, he walked through the garden. Finally, he gave water and fertilizer to the plants. Passages do not always come in a clear sequence. Sometimes they begin at the end. Or, they can start over at the beginning. You can strengthen your understanding of the passage by taking notes to understand the sequence.

Building a Vocabulary

Readers of all levels will find new words in passages. The best way to define a word in **context** is to think about the words that are around the unknown word. For example, nouns that you don't know may be followed by examples that give a definition. Think about this example: *Dave arrived at the party in hilarious garb: a leopard-print shirt, buckskin pants, and tennis shoes.* If you didn't know the meaning of garb, you could read the examples (i.e., a leopard-print shirt, buckskin pants, and tennis shoes) and know that *garb* means *clothing*. Examples will not always be this clear. Try another example: *Parsley, lemon, and flowers were just a few of the items he used as garnishes.* The word *garnishes* is explained by parsley, lemon, and flowers. From this one sentence, you may know that the items are used for decoration. Are they decorating a food plate or an ice table with meat? You would need the other sentences in the paragraph to know for sure.

> **Review Video: Context**
> Visit mometrix.com/academy and enter code: 613660

Also, you can use contrasts to define an unfamiliar word in context. In many sentences, authors will not describe the unfamiliar word directly. Instead, they will describe the opposite of the unfamiliar word. So, you are given some information that will bring you closer to defining the word. For example: *Despite his intelligence, Hector's bad posture made him look obtuse. Despite* means that Hector's posture is at odds with his intelligence. The author explains that Hector's posture does not prove his intelligence. So, *obtuse* must mean *unintelligent.* Another example: *Even with the horrible weather, we were beatific about our trip to Alaska.* The weather is described as *horrible.* So, *beatific* must mean something positive.

Sometimes, there will be very few context clues to help you define an unknown word. When this happens, **substitution** is a helpful tool. First, try to think of some synonyms for the words. Then, use those synonyms in place of the unknown words. If the passage makes sense, then the substitution has given some information about the unknown word. For example: *Frank's admonition rang in her ears as she climbed the mountain.* Don't know the definition of *admonition?* Then, try some substitutions: *vow, promise, advice, complaint,* or *compliment.* These words hint that an *admonition* is some sort of message. Once in a while substitution can get you a precise definition.

Usually, you can define an unfamiliar word by looking at the descriptive words in context. For example: *Fred dragged the recalcitrant boy kicking and screaming up the stairs.* The words *dragged, kicking,* and *screaming* all hint that the boy hates going up the stairs. So, you may think that *recalcitrant* means something like unwilling or protesting. In this example, an unfamiliar adjective was identified.

Description is used more to define an unfamiliar noun than unfamiliar adjectives. For example: *Don's wrinkled frown and constantly shaking fist labeled him as a curmudgeon.* Don is described as having a *wrinkled frown* and *constantly shaking fist.* This hints that a *curmudgeon* must be a grumpy, old man. Contrasts do not always give detailed information about the unknown word. However, they do give you some clues to understand the word.

Many words have more than one definition. So, you may not know how the word is being used in a sentence. For example, the verb *cleave* can mean *join* or *separate*. When you see this word, you need to pick the definition that makes the most sense. For example: *The birds cleaved together as they flew from the oak tree.* The use of the word *together* hints that *cleave* is being used to mean *join*. Another example: *Hermione's knife cleaved the bread cleanly.* A knife cannot join bread together. So, the word must hint at separation. Learning the purpose of a word with many meanings needs the same tricks as defining an unknown word. Look for context clues and think about the substituted words.

Figurative Language

When authors want to share their message in a creative way, they use figurative language devices. Learning these devices will help you understand what you read. **Figurative language** is communication that goes beyond the actual meaning of a word or phrase. **Descriptive language** that awakens imagery in the reader's mind is one type of figurative language. Exaggeration is another type of figurative language. Also, when you compare two things, you are using figurative language. Similes and metaphors are the two main ways of comparing things. An example of a simile: *The child howled like a coyote when her mother told her to pick up the toys.* In this example, the child's howling is compared to a coyote. This helps the reader understand the sound being made by the child.

A **figure of speech** is a word or phrase that is not a part of straightforward, everyday language. Figures of speech are used for emphasis, fresh expression, or clearness. However, clearness of a passage may be incomplete with the use of these devices. For example: *I am going to crown you.* The author may mean:

1. I am going to place a real crown on your head.
2. I am going to make you king or queen of this area.
3. I am going to punch you in the head with my fist.
4. I am going to put a second checker's piece on top of your checker piece to show that it has become a king.

> **Review Video: Figure of Speech**
> Visit mometrix.com/academy and enter code: 111295

Personification is the explanation of a nonhuman thing with human attributes. The basic purpose of personification is to describe something in a way that readers will understand. An author says that a tree *groans* in the wind. The author does not mean that the tree is giving a low, pained sound from a mouth.

However, the author means that the tree is making a noise like a human groan. Of course, this personification creates a tone of sadness or suffering. A different tone would be made if the author said that the tree *sways* or *dances*.

> **Review Video: Personification**
> Visit mometrix.com/academy and enter code: 260066

Irony is a statement that hints at the opposite of what you expect. In other words, the device is used when an author or character says one thing but means another. For example, imagine a man who is covered in mud and dressed in tattered clothes. He walks in his front door to meet his wife. Then, his wife asks him, "How was your day?" He says, "Great!" The man's response to his wife is an example of irony. There is a difference between irony and sarcasm. Sarcasm is similar to irony. However, sarcasm is hurtful for the person receiving the sarcastic statement. A sarcastic statement points to the foolishness of a person to believe that a false statement is true.

> **Review Video: <u>Irony</u>**
> Visit mometrix.com/academy and enter code: 374204

As you read, you will see more words in the context of a sentence. This will strengthen your vocabulary. Be sure to read on a regular basis. This practice will increase the number of ways that you have seen a word in context. Based on experience, a person can remember how a word was used in the past and use that knowledge for a new context. For example, a person may have seen the word *gull* used to mean a bird that is found near the seashore. However, a *gull* can be a person who is tricked easily. If the word in context is used for a person, you will see the insult. After all, gulls are not thought to be very smart. Use your knowledge of a word to find comparisons. This knowledge can be used to learn a new use of a word.

57

Essay

PRACTICE MAKES PREPARED WRITERS

Writing is a skill that continues to need development throughout a person's life. For some people, writing seems to be a natural gift. They rarely struggle with writer's block. When you read their papers, they have persuasive ideas. For others, writing is an intimidating task that they endure. As you practice, you can improve your skills and be better prepared for writing a time-sensitive essay.

A traditional way to prepare for the writing section is to read. When you read newspapers, magazines, and books, you learn about new ideas. You can read newspapers and magazines to become informed about issues that affect many people. As you think about those issues and ideas, you can take a position and form opinions. Try to develop these ideas and your opinions by sharing them with friends. After you develop your opinions, try writing them down as if you were going to spread your ideas beyond your friends.

Remember that you are practicing for more than an exam. Two of the most valuable skills in life are the abilities to **read critically** and to **write clearly**. When you work on evaluating the arguments of a passage and explain your thoughts well, you are developing skills that you will use for a lifetime. In this overview of essay writing, you will find strategies and tools that will prepare you to write better essays.

ESSAY OVERVIEW

For your exam you need to write an essay that shows your ability to understand and respond to an assignment. When you talk with others, you give beliefs, opinions, and ideas about the world around you. As you talk, you have the opportunity to share information with spoken words, facial expressions, or hand motions. If your audience seems confused about your ideas, you can stop and explain. However, when you write, you have a different assignment. As you write, you need to share information in a clear, precise way. Your readers will not have the chance to ask questions about your ideas. So, before you write your essay, you need to understand the assignment. As you write, you should be clear and precise about your ideas.

BRAINSTORM

Spend the first three to five minutes brainstorming for ideas. Write down any ideas that you might have on the topic. The purpose is to pull any helpful information from the depths of your memory. In this stage, anything goes down on note paper regardless of how good or bad the idea may seem at first glance. You may not bring your own paper for these notes. Instead, you will be provided with paper at the time of your test.

STRENGTH THROUGH DIFFERENT VIEWPOINTS

The best papers will contain several examples and mature reasoning. As you brainstorm, you should consider different perspectives. There are more than two sides to every topic. In an argument, there are countless perspectives that can be considered. On any topic, different groups are impacted and many reach the same conclusion or position. Yet, they reach the same conclusion through different paths. Before writing your essay, try to *see* the topic through as many different *eyes* as you can.

In addition, you don't have to use information on how the topic impacts others. You can draw from your own experience as you wish. If you prefer to use a personal narrative, then explain the experience and your emotions from that moment. Anything that you've seen in your community can be expanded upon to round out your position on the topic.

Once you have finished with your creative flow, you need to stop and review what you brainstormed. *Which idea allowed you to come up with the most supporting information?* Be sure to pick an angle that will allow you to have a thorough coverage of the prompt.

Every garden of ideas has weeds. The ideas that you brainstormed are going to be random pieces of information of different values. Go through the pieces carefully and pick out the ones that are the best. The best ideas are strong points that will be easy to write a paragraph in response.

Now, you have your main ideas that you will focus on. So, align them in a sequence that will flow in a smooth, sensible path from point to point. With this approach, readers will go smoothly from one idea to the next in a reasonable order. Readers want an essay that has a sense of continuity (i.e., Point 1 to Point 2 to Point 3 and so on).

START YOUR ENGINES

Now, you have a logical flow of the main ideas for the start of your essay. Begin by expanding on the first point, then move to your second point. Pace yourself. Don't spend too much time on any one of the ideas that you are expanding on. You want to have time for all of them. Make sure that you watch your time. If you have twenty minutes left to write out your ideas and you have four ideas, then you can only use five minutes per idea. Writing so much information in so little time can be an intimidating task. Yet, when you pace yourself, you can get through all of your points. If you find that you are falling behind, then you can remove one of your weaker arguments. This will allow you to give enough support to your remaining paragraphs.

Once you finish expanding on an idea, go back to your brainstorming session where you wrote out your ideas. You can scratch through the ideas as you write about them. This will let you see what you need to write about next and what you have left to cover.

Your introductory paragraph should have several easily identifiable features.

- First, the paragraph should have a quick description or paraphrasing of the topic. Use your own words to briefly explain what the topic is about.
- Second, you should list your writing points. What are the main ideas that you came up with earlier? If someone was to read only your introduction, they should be able to get a good summary of the entire paper.
- Third, you should explain your opinion of the topic and give an explanation for why you feel that way. What is your decision or conclusion on the topic?

Each of your following paragraphs should develop one of the points listed in the main paragraph. Use your personal experience and knowledge to support each of your points. Examples should back up everything.

Once you have finished expanding on each of your main points, you need to conclude your essay. Summarize what you written in a conclusion paragraph. Explain once more your argument on the prompt and review why you feel that way in a few sentences. At this stage, you have already backed up your statements. So, there is no need to do that again. You just need to refresh your readers on the main points that you made in your essay.

DON'T PANIC

Whatever you do during essay, do not panic. When you panic, you will put fewer words on the page and your ideas will be weak. Therefore, panicking is not helpful. If your mind goes blank when you see the prompt, then you need to take a deep breath. Force yourself to go through the steps listed above: brainstorm and put anything on scratch paper that comes to mind.

Also, don't get clock fever. You may be overwhelmed when you're looking at a page that is mostly blank. Your mind is full of random thoughts and feeling confused, and the clock is ticking down faster. You have already brainstormed for ideas. Therefore, you don't have to keep coming up with ideas. If you're running out of time and you have a lot of ideas that you haven't written down, then don't be afraid to make some cuts. Start picking the best ideas that you have left and expand on them. Don't feel like you have to write on all of your ideas.

A short paper that is well written and well organized is better than a long paper that is poorly written and poorly organized. Don't keep writing about a subject just to add sentences and avoid repeating a statement or idea that you have explained already. The goal is 1 to 2 pages of quality writing. That is your target, but you should not mess up your paper by trying to get there. You want to have a natural end to your work without having to cut something short. If your essay is a little long, then that isn't a problem as long as your ideas are clear and flow well from paragraph to paragraph. Just be sure that your writing stays inside the assigned borders of the papers. Remember to expand on the ideas that you identified in the brainstorming session.

Leave time at the end (at least three minutes) to go back and check over your work. Reread and make sure that everything you've written makes sense and flows well. Clean up any spelling or grammar mistakes. Also, go ahead and erase any brainstorming ideas that you weren't able to include. Then, clean up any extra information that you might have written that doesn't fit into your paper.

As you proofread, make sure that there aren't any fragments or run-ons. Check for sentences that are too short or too long. If the sentence is too short, then look to see if you have a specific subject and an active verb. If it is too long, then break up the long sentence into two sentences. Watch out for any "big words" that you may have used. Be sure that you are using difficult words correctly. Don't misunderstand; you should try to increase your vocabulary and use difficult words in your essay. However, your focus should be on developing and expressing ideas in a clear and precise way.

THE SHORT OVERVIEW

Depending on your preferences and personality, the essay may be your hardest or your easiest section. You are required to go through the entire process of writing a paper in a limited amount of time which is very challenging.

Stay focused on each of the steps for brainstorming. Go through the process of creative flow first. You can start by generating ideas about the prompt. Next, organize those ideas into a smooth flow. Then, pick out the ideas that are the best from your list.

Create a recognizable essay structure in your paper. Start with an introduction that explains what you have decided to argue. Then, choose your main points. Use the body paragraphs to touch on those main points and have a conclusion that wraps up the topic.

Save a few moments to go back and review what you have written. Clean up any minor mistakes that you might have made and make those last few critical touches that can make a huge difference. Finally, be proud and confident of what you have written!

Practice Test

Section 1 – Verbal Reasoning

Each of the following questions consists of one word followed by four words. Select the one word whose meaning is closest to the word in capital letters. You are not allowed to use scrap paper, a dictionary, or a thesaurus.

Part One – Synonyms

1. INSTRUCTOR
    a. dictator
    b. pupil
    c. survivor
    d. teacher

2. INSTANTLY
    a. definitely
    b. eventually
    c. immediately
    d. reluctantly

3. GIGANTIC
    a. harsh
    b. huge
    c. scary
    d. small

4. COSTLY
    a. attractive
    b. cheap
    c. expensive
    d. rare

5. FREQUENTLY
    a. difficulty
    b. easy
    c. freely
    d. often

6. OBSERVED
    a. hunted
    b. scared
    c. sold
    d. watched

7. PURCHASED

a. bargained
b. bought
c. complained
d. sold

8. ENTIRE

a. basic
b. divide
c. tired
d. whole

9. SUPERIOR

a. better
b. short
c. similar
d. weak

10. SELECTING

a. choosing
b. contacting
c. informing
d. locating

11. SWIFTLY

a. lightly
b. quickly
c. slowly
d. surely

12. CHUCKLED

a. chose
b. commented
c. helped
d. laughed

13. LOCATE

a. buy
b. enjoy
c. find
d. share

14. PUZZLED

a. admired
b. confused
c. retired
d. understand

15. CHEAP
   a. cheat
   b. cheer
   c. doubtfully
   d. inexpensive

16. INTELLIGENT
   a. mysterious
   b. nice
   c. pretty
   d. smart

17. REQUIRED
   a. needed
   b. studied
   c. wanted
   d. wished

Part Two – Sentence Completion

DIRECTIONS: Select the answer choice that best completes the sentence. You are not allowed to use scrap paper, a dictionary, or a thesaurus.

18. The pop star wore a disguise and exited through a back door to avoid being _____ by the paparazzi.
   a. humiliated
   b. ignored
   c. overlooked
   d. welcomed

19. The fashion expert _____ Sylvia's apparel as being out of date.
   a. applauded
   b. drafted
   c. praised
   d. rejected

20. The others were not upset by Steve's strange behavior, as they were _____ with it.
   a. acquainted
   b. appalled
   c. disgusted
   d. unfamiliar

21. Ned's clumsy handling of the garden hose caused poor little Ike to be _____.
   a. drenched
   b. dry
   c. entertained
   d. unaffected

22. That message I sent was intended _____ for you and not all of your friends.
   a. commonly
   b. expressly
   c. generally
   d. possibly

23. James exclaimed dramatically, "I'm so _____ that I could eat an immense meal!"
   a. congested
   b. nauseated
   c. satisfied
   d. starved

24. When he slid quietly out of his desk, the student _____ his things and left the room.
   a. collected
   b. delayed
   c. disciplined
   d. hoisted

25. When he discovered his fiancée's lies, his _____ reaction was to discount her request for trust.
   a. illegible
   b. instantaneous
   c. luscious
   d. unpredictable

26. The inventor found a(n) _____ method to resolve his product's design problem.
   a. awkward
   b. clever
   c. incompetent
   d. ingenuous

27. Glenda was _____ disability benefits because she had gainful employment.
   a. assigned
   b. given
   c. granted
   d. refused

28. Be forewarned that students who talk during her lectures particularly _____ this teacher.
   a. aid
   b. delight
   c. irritate
   d. soothe

29. Sue had _____ that the delicious meal would later give her digestive problems.
   a. anxieties
   b. diffused
   c. enshrined
   d. hopes

30. The low temperatures and high winds in the blizzard changed the difficult _____ for the campers.

    a. audition
    b. journey
    c. mortgage
    d. suffrage

31. How she could manipulate a child so shamelessly is _____ to me.

    a. admirable
    b. intolerable
    c. maternal
    d. prodigal

32. The discomfort you are feeling could be one of the _____ effects of your new medication.

    a. beneficial
    b. conflicting
    c. desirable
    d. useful

33. Accusations that the public figure was a(n) _____ man were, happily, proven to be false.

    a. commendable
    b. deceitful
    c. heroic
    d. pleasant

34. You can't be objective about your own work, so have a _____ third party look at it.

    a. biased
    b. disinterested
    c. prejudiced
    d. revolutionary

Section 2 – Quantitative Reasoning

In this section there are four possible answers after each question. Choose which one is best.

You are not allowed a calculator, a calculator watch, a ruler, a protractor, or a compass.

1. The figure shows an irregular quadrilateral and the lengths of its sides. Which of the following equations best shows the perimeter of the quadrilateral?

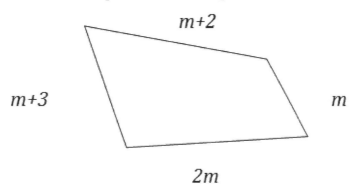

$m+2$

$m+3$

m

$2m$

    a. $m^4 + 5$
    b. $2m^4 + 5$
    c. $4m + 5$
    d. $5m + 5$

2. Of the 20 people in Joan's class, 4 of them have birthdays in the winter, 7 have birthdays in the spring, 3 have birthdays in the summer, and 6 have birthdays in the fall. What is the probability a student chosen at random will have a birthday in either the spring or the summer?

    a. $\dfrac{3}{20}$
    b. $\dfrac{3}{10}$
    c. $\dfrac{7}{20}$
    d. $\dfrac{1}{2}$

3. A rectangular plot in a garden is three times longer than it is wide. What is the perimeter of the garden if it has a width of 8 meters?

    a.   24 meters
    b.   32 meters
    c.   64 meters
    d.   192 meters

4. The figure below is divided into cubes. Each cube has a volume of 1 unit³. What is the volume of this figure?

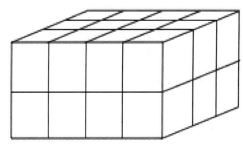

    a.   12 units
    b.   16 units
    c.   18 units
    d.   24 units

5. Which of the following correctly describes the relationship between the values of x and y, as shown in the table below?

x	y
1	4
2	8
3	12
4	16

    a.   The value of x is 6 less than the value of y
    b.   The value of y is 4 times the value of x
    c.   The value of y is 4 more than the value of x
    d.   The value of x is 1 less than the value of y

6. A bag full of C cookies is equally distributed among S students. Which expression correctly determines the number of cookies each student receives?

    a. $C \div S$
    b. $C \times S$
    c. $C - S$
    d. $S \div C$

7. Harlan plans to make stew for a large group. The recipe he uses requires 150 carrots. He knows that he can buy large bags of carrots for $3.75 each. What additional information does Harlan need to find the amount of money the carrots will cost for his stew?

    a.   The amounts of other vegetables he will need for the stew
    b.   The number of people he expects to eat the stew
    c.   The price each person attending the event paid
    d.   The number of carrots in a large bag of carrots

8. Which of the following is correct?

a. $\dfrac{4}{7} = \dfrac{12}{21}$

b. $\dfrac{3}{4} = \dfrac{12}{20}$

c. $\dfrac{5}{8} = \dfrac{15}{32}$

d. $\dfrac{7}{9} = \dfrac{28}{35}$

9. Aaron goes on a run every morning down the straight country road that he lives on. The graph below shows Aaron's distance from home at times throughout his morning run. Which of the following statements is (are) true?

I. Aaron's average running speed was 6 mph.

II. Aaron's running speed from point A to point B was the same as his running speed from point D to E.

III. Aaron ran a total distance of four miles.

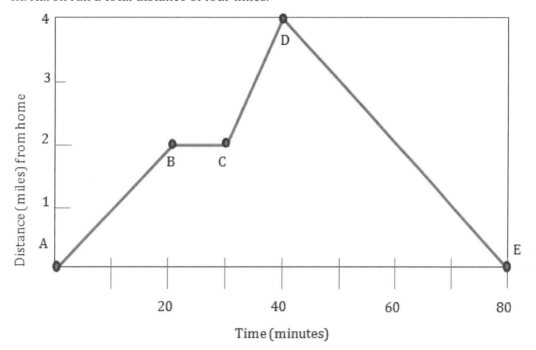

a. I only
b. II only
c. I and II
d. I, II, and III

10. An electronics store sells *E* Evercell brand batteries in packages of 4 and *D* Durapower brand batteries in packages of 6. Which expression represents the total number of batteries in the store?

a. $(4 + E) \times (6 + D)$
b. $(4 \times E) + (6 \times D)$
c. $(4 + E) + (6 + D)$
d. $(4 \times E) \div (6 \times D)$

11. A woman wants to park her 15 foot long car in a garage that is 19 feet long. How far from the front of the garage will her front wheels need to be so that the car is centered on the floor of the garage?

    a. 2 feet

    b. $2\frac{1}{2}$ feet

    c. 3 feet

    d. $3\frac{1}{2}$ feet

12. Two sets of numbers are shown here. In each set, the terms increase by the same amount each time.

        Set M = {1, 4, 7, 10, 13, ...}
        Set V = {1, 3, 5, 7, 9, ...}

What is the first number greater than 20 which is a member of both Set M and Set V?

    a. 21

    b. 23

    c. 25

    d. 27

13. Solve for x:

        4x + 4 = 36

    a. -11

    b. -8

    c. 5

    d. 8

14. Cindy earned \$100 one week at the ice cream stand. She put $\frac{1}{4}$ of the money in her savings account and kept the rest as cash. After this, she received a cash bonus of \$20 from the owner of the ice cream stand and didn't put any of it in the savings account. Which expression represents the amount of cash Cindy currently has?

    a. $C = \frac{3}{4}(100) + 20$

    b. $C = \frac{1}{4}(100) + 20$

    c. $C = \frac{1}{4}(100) - 2$

    d. $C = \frac{3}{4}(120)$

15. Which of the following shapes do not have a line symmetry?

    a.

    b.

    c.

    d.

16. Which one of the statements about the cube below is FALSE?

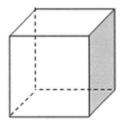

    a.   There are 12 edges on the cube.
    b.   All edges are the same length.
    c.   Some of the edges are parallel.
    d.   None of the edges are perpendicular.

17. Which statement about the shaded region of the two figures is true?
    a.   Figure A is greater than Figure B
    b.   Figure A is less than Figure B
    c.   Figure A is equal to figure B
    d.   No comparison can be made

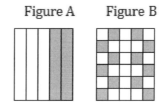

Figure A   Figure B

18. Jackson can decorate a cake in 3 hours. Eli can decorate the same cake in 2 hours. If they work together, how long will it take them to decorate the cake?
    a.   0.8 hours
    b.   1.2 hours
    c.   1.5 hours
    d.   1.8 hours

19. Two sisters were arguing who could have a larger piece of pie. Their mother told the older daughter she could have 2/5 of the pie. She told the younger daughter she could have 1/3 of the pie. Which daughter received a larger piece of pie?
    a.   The older daughter.
    b.   The younger daughter
    c.   Same size piece for each daughter
    d.   Not enough information to determine

20. A wealthy uncle decides to give away half of his fortune. Each of his 5 relatives is to receive an equal share. Which of the statements below describes how this can be done?
    a.   Multiply his wealth by 1/5 and give this amount to each of his relatives
    b.   Multiply his wealth by 1/2 and give this amount to each of his relatives
    c.   Multiply his wealth by 1/10 and give this amount to each of his relatives
    d.   Multiply his wealth by 2/5 and give this amount to each of his relatives

21. Which method below is NOT correct for finding the amount owed if three items are purchased at $3.99 each?

    a. $3 \times 4 - 3 \times 0.01$

    b. $3.99 \div 3$

    c. $3 \times 3 + 3 \times 0.9 + 3 \times 0.09$

    d. $3.99 + 3.99 + 3.99$

22. Which line is a line of symmetry for the figure?

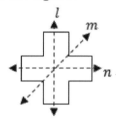

    a.   Line l

    b.   Line m

    c.   Line n

    d.   All of the above

23. Which of the following is the largest number?

    a.   0.004

    b.   0.400

    c.   0.2

    d.   0.03

24. The table below shows changes in the area of several trapezoids as the lengths of the bases, b_1 and b_2, remain the same and the height, h, changes.

Trapezoids

b_1 (in feet)	b_2 (in feet)	h (in feet)	A (in square feet)
5	7	2	12
5	7	4	24
5	7	6	36
5	7	8	48

Which formula best represents the relationship between A, the areas of these trapezoids, and h, their heights?

    a. $A = 5h$

    b. $A = 6h$

    c. $A = 7h$

    d. $A = 12h$

25. Alma collected coins. In the bag where she kept only dimes, she had dimes from four different years. She had 20 dimes minted in 1942, 30 minted in 1943, 40 minted in 1944, and 10 minted in 1945. If Alma reached into the bag without looking and took a dime, what is the probability that she took a dime minted in 1945?

   a. $\frac{1}{10}$

   b. $\frac{1}{5}$

   c. $\frac{3}{10}$

   d. $\frac{2}{5}$

26. Jason wants to put dry fertilizer on the grass in his front yard. The yard is 20 feet wide and 45 feet long. Each pound of the fertilizer he plans to use is enough for 150 square feet. Which procedure could Jason use to determine the correct amount of fertilizer to use on the entire yard?

   a. Divide 150 by 20 and divide 150 by 45, and then add those quotients together
   b. Add 20 and 45, double that total, and then divide that total by 150
   c. Multiply 20 by 45, and then subtract 150 from that product
   d. Multiply 20 by 45, and then divide that product by 150

27. Antonio wants to buy a roll of border to finish an art project. At four different shops, he found four different borders he liked. He wants to use the widest of the borders. The list shows the width, in inches, of the borders he found.

$$1\frac{7}{10}, 1.72, 1\frac{3}{4}, 1.695$$

Which roll of border should Antonio buy if he wants to buy the widest border?

   a. $1\frac{7}{10}$

   b. 1.72

   c. $1\frac{3}{4}$

   d. 1.695

28. Glenda poured salt into three salt shakers from a box that contained 26 ounces of salt. She poured 2 ounces of salt into one shaker, 3 ounces of salt into the second shaker, and 4 ounces into the third shaker. She did not pour salt into any other shakers. Which expression best represents the amount of salt left in the box after Glenda poured salt into the three shakers?

   a. 2 – 3 – 4 + 26
   b. 2 + 3 + 4 – 26
   c. 26 – 2 + 3 + 4
   d. 26 – 2 – 3 – 4

29. In ΔRST, shown here, m∠S is 20° less than m∠R.

What is the measure of ∠T?

    a. 20°
    b. 50°
    c. 70°
    d. 110°

30. The drawing shows a window with equal-sized panes. Some of the panes are not tinted, some are tinted a light shade of gray, and some are tinted a very dark shade of gray.

Which number sentence best models the total section of the window that has tinted panes?

    a. $\frac{1}{3} + \frac{1}{3} = \frac{2}{3}$
    b. $\frac{1}{3} + \frac{2}{9} = \frac{5}{9}$
    c. $\frac{1}{9} + \frac{2}{3} = \frac{7}{9}$
    d. $\frac{2}{9} + \frac{4}{9} = \frac{2}{3}$

31. Jeff saw 25 cars in the school parking lot. If each car brought from 1 to 3 people to school, which is the best estimate of the total number of people arriving to school in the 25 cars?

    a. 25
    b. 50
    c. 75
    d. 100

32. One morning at Jim's café, 25 people ordered juice, 10 ordered milk, and 50 ordered coffee with breakfast. Which ratio best compares the number of people who ordered milk to the number of people who ordered juice?

    a. 5 to 7
    b. 5 to 2
    c. 2 to 7
    d. 2 to 5

33. A unit of liquid measure in the English System of Measure is the gill. The table, shown here, gives conversions from gills to fluid ounces.

Conversion Table

Gills	Fluid Ounces
2	8
4	16
5	20
6	24
10	40

Which equation best describes the relationship between gills, g, and fluid ounces, f?

   a. $f = 8g - 8$
   b. $f = 2g + 4$
   c. $f = 4g$
   d. $4f = g$

34. A trash company charges a fee of $80 to haul off a load of trash. There is also a charge of $0.05 per mile the load must be hauled. Which equation can be used to find c, the cost for hauling a load of trash m miles?

   a. $80(m + 0.05)$
   b. $0.05(m + 80)$
   c. $80m + 0.05$
   d. $0.05m + 80$

35. Which of these is NOT a net of a cube?

  a.   b.   c.   d.

   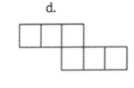

36. Which of the following statements is true?

   a. The measure of an acute angle is greater than the measure of a right angle, but less than the measure of an obtuse angle
   b. The measure of a right angle is greater than the measure of an acute angle, but less than the measure of an obtuse angle
   c. The measure of an obtuse angle is less than the measure of a right angle, but greater than the measure of an acute angle
   d. The measure of an obtuse angle is less than the measure of an acute angle, but greater than the measure of a right angle

37. The number of customers in a new restaurant is given in the table below:

Week	Customers
1	155
2	180
3	205

How many customers should be expected in week 4?

 a. 200
 b. 225
 c. 230
 d. 255

38. An elevator leaves the first floor of a 25-story building with 3 people on board. It stops at every floor. Each time it comes to an even-numbered floor, 3 people get on and one person gets off. Each time it comes to an odd-numbered floor, 3 people get on and 4 people get off. How many people are on board when it arrives at the 25th floor?

 a. 12
 b. 13
 c. 15
 d. 16

Section 3 – Reading Comprehension

You are not allowed to use scrap paper, a dictionary, or a thesaurus.

The Tournament

The Knights led by two points, and Scott was just outside the three-point line. If he could make the shot, the Eagles would be state champions again. But if he missed ... Scott
5 didn't want to think about that. He knew what he had to do. It was a classic jump shot. The ball left his hands and sailed toward the basket in a perfect arc. The crowd and the other players seemed frozen in time. All eyes
10 were on the ball as it struck the rim and bounced off. The buzzer blared. The game was over. Scott had missed, and the Eagles had lost.

Scott stood like a statue on the court as
15 people surged around him. Family members swarmed the winning team. Teammates hugged and patted each other on the back. Local reporters gathered around the Knights head coach for a comment and a photograph.

20 Suddenly, Scott realized that he was being hoisted onto the shoulders of his friends. Over the loudspeaker, the announcer had proclaimed that Scott had been named the most valuable player of the championship
25 game. Everyone was elated, and the Eagles took a victory lap with Scott on their shoulders.

Scott was confused as his teammates set him down. He was the one who missed the most
30 important shot of the game. How could anyone call him the most valuable player? He didn't feel very valuable at the moment. Scott approached Coach Travis. "Coach," Scott said,

"there must be some mistake. I can't be the
35 most valuable player."

"There's no mistake," Coach Travis said. "You had 26 points, 11 rebounds, and 8 assists. I'd say that makes you a very valuable player."

"But I missed that last shot," Scott said. "We
40 lost the game because of me."

"I don't know about that," said Coach Travis. "Everybody misses a shot from time to time. Don't be so hard on yourself. It's all depends on how you look at the outcome."

45 "What do you mean?" Scott asked.

"Well," Coach Travis answered, "you could say you are the reason we lost the game because you missed that shot. On the other hand, you could say you are the reason we
50 almost won because of your performance throughout the game. How you look at it is up to you."

Scott's teammates came running over and surrounded Coach Travis. "Hey, Coach," one
55 player called out, "how about treating your team to pizza?"

"I don't know," said Coach Travis. "Do you think you deserve pizza?"

Scott piped up. "Of course we do! After all, we
60 almost won the game."

Coach Travis smiled. "You're right, Scott. We did almost win. Okay. Pizza for everyone!"

1. In line 25, what does "elated" mean?
a. Happy and excited
b. Frustrated and angry
c. Loud and rowdy
d. Pushy and proud

2. In line 14, what type of figurative language is used?

    a. Hyperbole
    b. Metaphor
    c. Personification
    d. Simile

3. Which of the following best expresses the theme of this story?

    a. The Eagles want to be the state champions
    b. There are different ways to look at any situation
    c. Winning isn't everything
    d. Scott is a very good basketball player

4. Which of the following is the best summary of this story?

    a. At the buzzer, Scott misses an important basket because he isn't a very good basketball player
    b. Coach Travis feels Scott is the most valuable player in the game because he scored 26 points
    c. When Scott misses an important shot, he is disappointed, but Coach Travis shows him there are different ways to look at the situation
    d. The Eagles lose the state championship because of Scott, but Coach Travis sees things differently and makes Scott the most valuable player

5. Why is Scott so upset in this story?

    a. He feels responsible for losing the game
    b. He thinks he is a bad basketball player
    c. He doesn't like Coach Travis
    d. He doesn't want to play basketball anymore

The Tradition of Dance

It is estimated that there are over 300 Native American tribes, and each of them uses dancing to communicate culture. Native American dances date back hundreds of years
5 and come in many different forms. Different tribes use dance for different purposes and to convey different messages.

Although each dance is different, they all have meanings that are rooted in ancient tradition.
10 The Iroquois performed a corn husk dance to bring good crops and many healthy babies to the tribe. The Choctaw women danced with medicine men to bring their tribe victory in sporting events. The Plains Indians offered
15 thanks to the gods through their Sun Dance, and the Cherokee celebrated both peace and war with the Eagle Dance. During the Snake Ceremonial, Hopi dancers even held live snakes in their mouths before releasing them
20 into the desert to bring rain and a good harvest.

Each of the many different dances also requires a unique costume. These costumes vary widely, but—just like the dances—each
25 has a special meaning. Most dance costumes include a headdress and special ceremonial clothing. Some also include a wand, jewelry, and even body paint. In addition, feathers are often used in costumes to symbolize human
30 traits. One of the most common feathers used is the eagle feather, which represents strength in many tribes.

Though many of the Native American dances are now performed only in ceremonies and at
35 powwows, they remain an important element of Native American culture. These dances are a language, rich in history and meaning. They are passed from generation to generation and will always be a vital part of Native American
40 tradition.

6. What is the main purpose of dance in the Native American culture?
   a. To provide exercise
   b. To communicate a message
   c. To entertain children
   d. To prepare for battle

7. According to paragraph 2 (lines 8–32), what is the similarity between the Iroquois corn husk dance and the Hopi Snake Ceremonial?
   a. They were both intended to bring good crops
   b. They both involved women and medicine men
   c. They both involved the use of snakes
   d. They both involved the use of corn husks

8. Which of the following is a statement of fact?
   a. Eagle feathers are the best feathers
   b. Native American costumes are beautiful
   c. Ceremonial headdresses make dancers look important
   d. Many Native American costumes include a wand and jewelry

9. What does the eagle feather represent in many Native American tribes?
   a. Power
   b. Wealth
   c. Strength
   d. Authority

10. What was the author's main purpose in writing this article?

    a. To inform
    b. To entertain
    c. To influence
    d. To persuade

<u>The Giant Sequoia</u>

Most people think that the Giant Sequoia (*Sequoiadendron giganteum*) is the largest living organism. This conifer grows mostly in groves located in the Sierra Nevada
5 Mountains in California. The biggest single Giant Sequoia is called the General Sherman tree. The General Sherman is 250 feet tall and has a diameter of 24.75 feet at the bottom. The trunk of this massive tree weighs nearly
10 1400 tons. That's about the weight of 10 trains or 15 fully grown blue whales.

But some people do not think that labeling the Giant Sequoia as the largest living organism is correct. That is because the
15 majority of the material that makes up a tree is made up of dead cells rather than living matter. In addition, there are other types of plants that reproduce in such a way that they are connected with roots under the ground,
20 such as a grove of aspen trees or a field of goldenrod flowers. Some people think that these large, connected groves should be considered the largest organism. In any case, a Giant Sequoia is indeed a massive and
25 beautiful sight to behold indeed.

11. Based on the context of this passage, what is a conifer?

    a. an animal
    b. a tree
    c. a flower
    d. a cell

12. Is the Giant Sequoia the largest organism?

    a. yes
    b. no
    c. some people think it is
    d. most people think so

13. What is the General Sherman?

    a. the biggest train
    b. the largest connected organism
    c. the largest Giant Sequoia
    d. a type of whale

14. Why do some people think that a grove of aspen trees should be considered the largest organism?

    a. because the trees are taller
    b. because the trees have a wider diameter
    c. because the grove is connected underneath the ground
    d. because there are more of them in the United States

15. What is the diameter of the General Sherman tree at the top?

    a.   15 feet
    b.   20 feet
    c.   24.75 feet
    d.   This question cannot be answered from the information given

<u>Remember the Alamo</u>

In the early 1700s, the Spanish established missions throughout the land we now know as the state of Texas. One of the most famous of these missions was San Antonio de Valero, better known by its nickname: the Alamo. This was the most successful mission in the area, and it served a number of purposes for the surrounding communities.

For over a century, the Alamo served as an active mission. Church services were held in the cool, shady buildings, providing welcome relief from the blazing summer sun. Couples were married at the Alamo. Babies were baptized there. The Alamo also served as a trading post, supply depot, and communication center. In later years, however, the Alamo served its most famous and—arguably—most important role; it was a fortress for freedom fighters.

During the 1830s, Texas was in a battle for independence from Mexico, which owned it at that time. This struggle came to a head in 1836 when 184 Texans, led by William Travis, holed up in the Alamo. Travis and other famous American fighters—including Jim Bowie and Davy Crockett—fought side by side with farmers, ranchers, cowboys, and businessmen. Those brave men held off Mexican General Santa Anna's army for 13 days from the secure walls of the Alamo.

Finally, in the gray, early morning light of March 6, 1836, General Santa Anna and an army of 4,000 soldiers overran the Alamo. Every man in the Alamo died that day, but their ability to hold out for nearly two weeks gave American General Sam Houston the time he needed to assemble a more substantial army. General Houston soon defeated General Santa Anna, and Texas won its independence, thanks in great part to the brave men who defended the Alamo and the cause of freedom.

16. What was the official name of the mission nicknamed "the Alamo"?

    a.   San Antonio de Valente
    b.   San Antonio de Verde
    c.   San Antonio de Valero
    d.   San Antonio de Vallejo

17. Which of the following represents the author's main purpose in writing this story?

    a.   To inform
    b.   To influence
    c.   To entertain
    d.   To persuade

18. What was the main motivation for the men who fought at the Alamo?

    a.   Wealth
    b.   Fame
    c.   Safety
    d.   Freedom

19. Based on the information in paragraph 2 (lines 9–19), what was the purpose of the Alamo?

    a. It was designed as a war fortress
    b. It was designed to serve many purposes in the community
    c. It was designed as a trading post
    d. It was designed as a saloon

20. Which of the following is a statement of opinion?

    a. William Travis, Davy Crockett, and Jim Bowie fought at the Alamo
    b. All the men who fought to defend the Alamo died in the battle
    c. General Santa Anna was eventually defeated by General Sam Houston
    d. General Santa Anna was a better leader than William Travis

Cultivation of Tomato Plants

Tomato plants should be started in window boxes or greenhouses in late March so that they will be ready for the garden after the last frost. Use a soil of equal parts of sand, peat
5 moss and manure, and plant the seeds about a quarter of an inch deep. After covering, water them through a cloth to protect the soil and cover the box with a pane of glass. Keep the box in a warm place for a few days, then
10 place it in a sunny window. After the second leaf makes its appearance on the seedling, transplant the plant to another box, placing the seedlings two inches apart. Another alternative is to put the sprouted seedlings in
15 four-inch pots, setting them deeper in the soil than they stood in the seed bed. To make the stem stronger, pinch out the top bud when the seedlings are four or five inches in height.

Finally, place the plants in their permanent
20 positions after they have grown to be twelve or fifteen inches high. When transplanting, parts of some of the longest leaves should be removed. Large plants may be set five or six inches deep.

25 The soil should be fertilized the previous season. Fresh, stable manure, used as fertilizer, would delay the time of fruiting. To improve the condition of the soil, work in a spade full of old manure to a depth of at least
30 a foot. Nitrate of soda, applied at about two hundred pounds per acre, may be used to give the plant a good start. Plants grown on supports may be set two feet apart in the row, with the rows three or four feet apart
35 depending upon the variety. Plants not supported by stakes or other methods should be set four feet apart.

Unsupported vines give a lighter yield and much of the fruit is likely to rot during the
40 wet seasons. Use well sharpened stakes about two inches in diameter and five feet long. Drive the stakes into the ground at least six inches from the plants so that the roots will not be injured. Tie the tomato vines to the
45 stakes with strings made out of strips of cloth, as twine is likely to cut them. Care must be taken not to wrap the limbs so tightly as to interfere with their growth. The training should start before the plants begin to trail on
50 the ground.

21. What is the overall purpose of this passage?

    a. To describe how soil should be treated in order to plant tomatoes.
    b. To give an overview of how tomato plants are cultured.
    c. To teach the reader how to operate a farm.
    d. To describe a method of supporting tomato vines.

22. According to the passage, why is late March the best time to germinate tomato seeds?
   a. The last frost has already passed by this time.
   b. It is warm enough by then to germinate them in window boxes.
   c. By the time the last frost passes, they will be ready to transplant outdoors.
   d. The seeds might not be fertile if one were to wait longer.

23. What does the passage imply as the reason that the seeds not planted outdoors immediately?
   a. A late freeze might kill the seedlings.
   b. The soil outdoors is too heavy for new seedlings.
   c. A heavy rain might wash away the seedlings.
   d. New seedlings need to be close to one another and then be moved apart later.

24. What would happen if the bud weren't pinched out of the seedlings when they are in individual pots?
   a. The plants would be weaker.
   b. The plants would freeze.
   c. The plants would need more water.
   d. The plants would not survive as long.

25. What is the purpose of the last paragraph?
   a. To explain why unsupported plants give rotten fruit.
   b. To explain why cloth is used rather than wire.
   c. To describe in detail how tomato plants are cultured.
   d. To instruct the reader in the method of supporting tomato vines for culture.

Section 4 – Mathematics Achievement

In this section there are four possible answers after each question. Choose which one is best. You are not allowed a calculator, a calculator watch, a ruler, a protractor, or a compass.

1. Janice gets home from school at 2:45 PM. She does homework for 1 hour and 30 minutes, then goes out and plays for 1 hour and 45 minutes before returning home for dinner. What time is it when Janice returns home for dinner?

a.

b.

c.

d.

2. What is the value of the digit 5 in the number 3,456,789?

    a. Fifty thousand
    b. Five thousand
    c. Five-hundred thousand
    d. Five million

3. What is the 14ᵗʰ number in the pattern shown below?

        100, 200, 300, 400, ...

    a. 1,200
    b. 1,300
    c. 1,400
    d. 1,500

4. The recipe Mary is using to bake cupcakes requires 1 cup of milk and makes 8 cupcakes. If she needs to make 32 cupcakes for the party, how much milk is needed?

    a. 1 pint
    b. 1 gallon
    c. 3 cups
    d. 1 quart

5. Matthew wants to buy a video game that costs $25. He only has $18. How much additional money does Matthew need to save to purchase the game?

    a. $5
    b. $6
    c. $7
    d. $8

6. Julie shopped for first-aid cream. One large tube held 1.5 fluid ounces and the smallest tube held 0.33 fluid ounces. What is the difference in the number of fluid ounces of cream in the two tubes?

    a. 1.17
    b. 1.23
    c. 1.27
    d. 1.8

7. 3.5 + 10.3 + 0.63 =

    a. 11.28
    b. 13.58
    c. 14.43
    d. 20.10

8. Large boxes of canned beans hold 24 cans of beans and small boxes hold 12 cans. One afternoon, Gerald brought 4 large boxes of canned beans and 6 small boxes of canned beans to the food bank. How many cans of beans did Gerald bring to the food bank that afternoon?

    a. 168
    b. 192
    c. 288
    d. 360

9. Enrique used a formula to find the total cost, in dollars, for repairs he and his helper, Jenny, made to a furnace. The expression below shows the formula he used, with 4 being the number of hours he worked on the furnace and 2 being the number of hours Jenny worked on the furnace.

$$20 + 35(4 + 2) + 47$$

What is the total cost for repairing the furnace?

    a. $189
    b. $269
    c. $277
    d. $377

10. What is the equivalent decimal number for six hundred six thousandths?

    a. .0606

    b. .606

    c. 6.006

    d. 6.600

11. Jan played a game which used a fair spinner like the one shown here. Jan needs the arrow to land on green on her next turn.

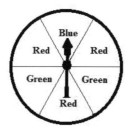

What is the probability that the arrow lands on green when Jan spins one time?

    a. $\frac{1}{6}$

    b. $\frac{1}{3}$

    c. $\frac{1}{2}$

    d. $\frac{2}{3}$

12. What decimal is represented by Point P, shown on the number line below?

    a. 5.6

    b. 5.7

    c. 5.8

    d. 5.9

13. Simplify $4\frac{1}{3} - 2\frac{2}{3}$.

    a. $1\frac{1}{9}$

    b. $1\frac{2}{3}$

    c. $2\frac{1}{3}$

    d. $2\frac{3}{6}$

14. Stephen researched the topic of solar-powered lights for his science project. He exposed 10 new solar lights to five hours of sunlight. He recorded the number of minutes each light continued to shine after dark in the list below.

$$63, 67, 73, 75, 80, 91, 63, 72, 79, 87$$

Which of these numbers is the mean of the number of minutes in Stephen's list?

    a. 28
    b. 63
    c. 74
    d. 75

15. Petra installed 10 light fixtures at a new warehouse that was being built. Each of the fixtures required 3 light bulbs. The bulbs come in packages of 5 and cost $8 per package. What was the total cost for the bulbs required for all of the fixtures Petra installed at the warehouse?

    a. $16
    b. $48
    c. $120
    d. $240

16. Where would the answer to $\frac{4}{5} - \frac{1}{16}$ lie on the number line below?

    a. between 0 and $\frac{1}{4}$
    b. between $\frac{1}{4}$ and $\frac{1}{2}$
    c. between $\frac{1}{2}$ and $\frac{3}{4}$
    d. between $\frac{3}{4}$ and 1

17. What type of transformation is represented by the two figures below?

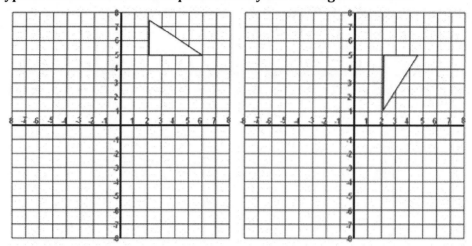

a. Reflection
b. Translation
c. Rotation
d. None of these

18. Which of the following is the written form for the number 5,320,080?
a. five million, thirty-two thousand, eighty
b. five million, three hundred twenty thousand, eighty
c. five million, three hundred twenty thousand, eight
d. five thousand, three hundred twenty-eight

19. Round 514, 684. 51 to the thousands place.
a. 510,000.00
b. 514,000.00
c. 515,000.00
d. 520,000.00

20. A large rectangular-prism-shaped tank at the zoo is 8 feet wide and 5 feet high. How long is the tank if it holds a volume of 200 cubic feet of water?
a. 5 feet
b. 6 feet
c. 8 feet
d. 13 feet

21. Mr. Aguilera needs 71 feet of fencing that costs $3.98 per foot. Which is the best approximation for the price of the fencing?
a. $210
b. $240
c. $280
d. $320

22. A ship is located on the map at coordinates (4, 9). If the radar indicates the lighthouse is 5 units east and 4 units south of the ship, what is the location of the lighthouse?

North

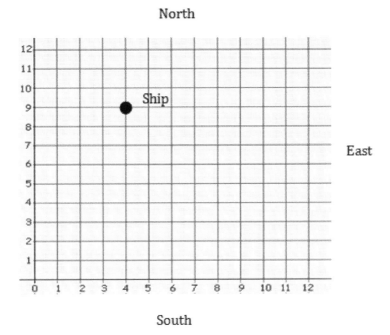

East

South

   a.   (9, 5)
   b.   (9, 4)
   c.   (8, 3)
   d.   (9, 13)

23. The side length of a regular pentagon is 6.5 centimeters. What is the perimeter of this figure?

   a.   26.0 cm
   b.   32.5 cm
   c.   39.0 cm
   d.   42.25 cm

24. The length of the football field near Gerald's school is 120 yards. What is the length of the field in feet?

   a.   12 feet
   b.   360 feet
   c.   400 feet
   d.   1,440 feet

25. Evan measured the amount of rain in the gauge over the weekend. On Saturday, he measured $1\frac{6}{10}$ inches and on Sunday, $\frac{8}{10}$ inches. What is the total amount of rain, in inches, Evan measured on those two days, written in the simplest form?

    a. $1\frac{2}{5}$

    b. $1\frac{4}{10}$

    c. $1\frac{14}{20}$

    d. $2\frac{2}{5}$

26. Given the isosceles trapezoid PQRS below, which two sides are congruent?

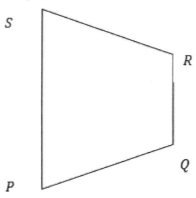

    a. $\overline{PS}$ and $\overline{QR}$
    b. $\overline{RS}$ and $\overline{QP}$
    c. $\overline{QP}$ and $\overline{RQ}$
    d. $\overline{PS}$ and $\overline{RS}$

27. William needs to find the value of the expression below. What is the value of this expression?

        $40 - 4(3 - 1)$

    a. 29
    b. 32
    c. 72
    d. 107

28. Annette read that out of 20 televisions sold in her state last year, 3 were Brand V. If a furniture store near her home sold 360 televisions last year, about how many should Annette expect to be Brand V?

    a. 18
    b. 54
    c. 1,080
    d. 2,400

29. Curtis measured the temperature of water in a flask in Science class. The temperature of the water was 35°C. He carefully heated the flask so that the temperature of the water increased about 2°C every 3 minutes. Approximately how much had the temperature of the water increased after 20 minutes?

    a.   10°C
    b.   13°C
    c.   15°C
    d.   35°C

30. Express the calculation "subtract 4 from 18, then divide by 7."

    a. $(4 - 18) \div 7$
    b. $4 - 18 \div 7$
    c. $(18 - 4) \div 7$
    d. $18 - 4 \div 7$

Section 5 – Essay

Write an essay on the following prompt on the paper provided. Your essay should NOT exceed 2 pages and must be written in blue or black ink. You are not allowed to use scrap paper, a dictionary, or a thesaurus.

Prompt: <u>Should public schools be allowed to sell junk food such as chips and soda?</u>

Support your position with specific examples from personal experience, the experience of others, current events, history, or literature.

Answers and Explanations

Section 1: Verbal Reasoning

1. D: A teacher provides instruction and information to an individual or group of individuals. An instructor functions in the same capacity, that is, in the practice of teaching.

2. C: To say something was done instantly means that it was done immediately and without hesitation.

3. B: Something that is described as gigantic is extremely large, or huge, in size.

4. C: Something that is costly is expensive because it costs a lot of money.

5. D: To say that something is done frequently implies that it is done regularly or often.

6. D: Something that is being observed is being watched. Binoculars are used to see things more clearly, so it makes sense that the man would be observing or watching eagles with binoculars.

7. B: Saying that somebody purchased something and saying they bought something conveys the same meaning.

8. D: Entire is an amount. It usually means the whole amount. For example, if someone says they ate an entire apple, it is the same as saying they ate a whole apple.

9. A: To say something is superior to something else usually implies that it is better.

10. A: When a selection is being made, it involves making a choice between several options. Selecting something is the same as choosing something.

11. B: When something is done swiftly, it means that it is done fast or quickly.

12. D: Chuckled is a synonym for laughed. To say somebody chuckled or to say that somebody laughed conveys the same meaning.

13. C: To locate something that is lost or misplaced is to find it. For example, the child could not locate (find) his toy.

14. B: If somebody is puzzled about something, it implies confusion or bewilderment. For example, to say that a man was puzzled by the woman's reaction means that the man was confused by her reaction.

15. D: Something that is cheap does not cost a substantial amount of money. Saying something is cheap and saying that something is inexpensive conveys the same meaning.

16. D: When somebody is described as intelligent, it usually means that they are smart.

17. A: Something that is required is needed. For example, if you say you require ten dollars to buy lunch, it implies that you need ten dollars for lunch.

18. A: Humiliated means embarrassment or hurting someone's self-respect. Since the star is wearing a disguise, it is unlikely that the star fears being overlooked (C) or ignored (B). Instead, the

93

star does not want to get their attention. The evasive tactics are to avoid being noticed or humiliated by their attention. Being welcomed (D) carries a positive connotation and is thus less likely to be avoided.

19. D: A fashion expert's identifying something as out-of-date would be negative, not a compliment. So, the expert would not applaud Sylvia's clothing (A) or praise her accessories (C), which both have positive connotations. The verb drafted (B) means that someone or something is chosen from a group. Drafting can also refer to someone who has started to write a paper or started to put together a plan.

20. A: The others were acquainted with—i.e., knew about or were familiar with—Steve's strange behavior and thus were not upset by it. Appalled (B) and disgusted (C) are synonyms meaning that they certainly were upset with the behavior. However, this would contradict the sentence's statement that they were not upset. Unfamiliar (D) is an antonym of acquainted. While unfamiliarity with some things could prevent someone from being upset about them, this sentence describes Steve's behavior as strange, which is more likely to upset people who are unfamiliar with it than those who are used to it.

21. A: The description of "poor little" Ike implies that Ned's handling of the hose caused something unfortunate and unintended to happen to Ike, like being drenched with water, which could be caused by clumsy handling. So, the context of the sentence does not suggest that Ike was entertained (C). If the handling of the hose was clumsy, then this would not cause Ike to stay dry (B) because it does not explain why he is "poor little" Ike. Again, the context of the sentence does suggest that Ike was unaffected (D) because nothing good seems to have happened to Ike.

22. B: Expressly means specifically, particularly, especially, precisely, exactly. Generally (C) and commonly (A) are antonyms of expressly. Possibly (D), meaning not definitely/not surely, is also an antonym of expressly, precisely, exactly.

23. D: Starved means very hungry. So, if James is famished, he could eat an immense, i.e., very large, meal. Nauseated (B) means sick. So, if James were not well, he could not eat an immense meal. Congested (A) means overly full or stuffed. If James exclaimed that he was congested, he probably would not be interested in any kind of meal. Also, if James were satisfied (C), then he would obviously not be interested in a meal.

24. A: Collected means gather, group, or accumulate. The context of the sentence tells us that the student does not want to be a distraction. So, the student would not hoist (D) (i.e., raise or lift) his things into the air before leaving the classroom. Discipline (C) means to instruct or to order and is reserved for people or animals, not things like classroom materials. Choice B is not the correct choice because the word delay suggests being late and classroom materials cannot be late.

25. B: Instantaneous means immediate, in an instant, right away. To discount her means to dismiss or ignore. Illegible (A) means that someone's writing or print is very difficult to read or understand. Luscious (C) means that something is delicious or sweet which does not make sense in this sentence. Unpredictable (D) means changeable, erratic, unreliable, and unforeseeable and could be an adjective with "his reaction." However, to discount her for lying is a predictable reaction.

26. B: Clever means brilliant, perceptive, able, and skilled. Since the method the inventor found resolved his product's design problem, it is logical that it was clever. Ingenuous (D) means honest, trusting, and sincere. Incompetent (C) and awkward (A) mean unskillful or inadequate and are antonyms of clever.

27. D: Refused means not allowed, rejected, denied. Gainful means profitable, productive, lucrative, money-making. If Glenda has gainful employment, she will be denied disability benefits, which are given to applicants who are disabled from any gainful employment. So Glenda would not be granted (C), given (B), or assigned (A) disability benefits for having employment.

28. C: To irritate means to annoy, aggravate, or upset. Since the sentence begins with a warning and since the student behavior of talking during lectures is generally an unpopular one with teachers, this choice fits best in the sentence. To delight (B), or please, to aid (A), or help, and to soothe (D), or calm, are all opposites of irritate, hence do not fit the sentence meaning.

29. A: Anxieties are worries, fears, doubts, and apprehensions. Delicious is an adjective that can describe a meal and later digestive problems certainly can be worthy of anxieties. Diffuse (B) as a verb means that something is spread out which does not fit the context of this sentence. When someone or something is enshrined (C), the person or object is marked as important and should not be harmed. So, this does not fit the context of the sentence. An antonym of anxieties is hopes (D) which is very unlikely for someone in this situation.

30. B: A blizzard is a snow storm that lasts for several hours with high winds and freezing temperatures. So, this kind of storm would delay a journey for people who wanted to camp during the winter. The campers are not auditioning (A) (i.e., a try out or interview) for a position. Also, the campers would not be concerned about a mortgage (C) (i.e., a type of loan that people use to purchase a house). Suffrage (D) is the right to vote which would not be concern for campers facing a blizzard.

31. B: The adverb shamelessly means that someone shows no regret or sadness about a wrong action. To manipulate someone is to use, control, maneuver, deceive, take advantage of that person. The action of manipulating a child is one that should be seen as intolerable which means unacceptable. Also, the witness of the event clearly thinks that this is not acceptable behavior by calling it shameless. So, the witness would not think of it as admirable (A) which means excellent or respectful. A maternal (C) action is one that is kind, protective, and reminds others of good mothers. However, this is not the case for a shameless action on a child. Finally, prodigal (D) is an adjective that describes a foolish waste of time or money. So, this does not fit the context of this sentence.

32. B: Conflicting means opposing or clashing, so feeling discomfort would be a conflicting effect of a medication. Beneficial (A) is an antonym of conflicting and refers to that which is positive, favorable, helpful. Desirable (C) means wanted or healthful, a synonym of beneficial, as is useful (D). These are all positive adjectives and are inconsistent with the negative effect of feeling discomfort.

33. B: A deceitful person says one thing but does another. The word carries a negative connotation that is consistent with an accusation, i.e., a charge of wrongdoing. Accusations would be "happily" proven false. Accusations are not made about a hero (C), who is a positive figure. Also, a public figure would not happily want claims of heroism to be proven false. Accusations do not fit someone who is commendable (A), meaning someone who is respected or worthy of praise. Calling someone a commendable person would not be "happily" proven false. Again, a pleasant (D) man is someone who is kind and gentle. These admirable qualities would want to be proven true.

34. B: A disinterested third party is one that is detached or uninvolved in the work mentioned. Prejudiced (C), literally meaning prejudging, without knowledge or basis, is an antonym of disinterested. Revolutionary (D), meaning radical or rebellious does not fit the context of the sentence. After all, a rebellious and radical person may not be the best person to give disinterested feedback. Biased (A), meaning slanted, inclined, distorted, is an antonym of disinterested.

Section 2: Quantitative Reasoning

1. D: The perimeter (P) of the quadrilateral is simply the sum of its sides:

$$P = m + (m + 2) + (m + 3) + 2m$$

Put together like terms by adding the variables (m terms) together. Then, add the constants. This gives you: $P = 5m + 5$

In this problem, it seems that some of the variables do not have a number in front of them. However, when there is no coefficient, this means multiplication by 1. So, $m = 1m$, $x = 1x$, and so on.

2. D: Since the probability of being born in the spring or summer is being calculated, the probabilities are added. $\frac{7}{20} + \frac{3}{20} = \frac{10}{20} = \frac{1}{2}$.

3. C: A diagram of the plot would look like this:

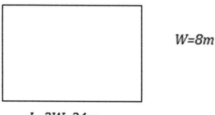

W=8m

L=3W=24 m

The perimeter of a rectangle is the formula $P = 2L + 2W$ which produces $2(24) + 2(8) = 48 + 16 = 64\ m$.

4. D: To find the volume of the rectangular prism, find the number of cubes in the figure. The figure has two layers of cubes. On the top layer, the number of cubes can be counted. There are 12 cubes on the top layer. The bottom layer is the same as the top, so there are also 12 cubes in the bottom layer. There are 24 total cubes in the figure, so the volume of the figure is 24 units³.

5. B: The value of y is indeed 4 times the value of x. Note. 4 is 4 times the value of 1; 8 is 4 times the value of 2; 12 is 4 times the value of 3; and 16 is 4 times the value of 4.

6. A: $C \div S$. Since the cookies are being divided up equally between the S students. Use some numbers to help see the correct answer. If $C = 40$ and $S = 10$.

$$C \div S = 40 \div 10 = 4$$

The incorrect choices produce the following with these values:

$$C \times S = 40 \times 10 = 400$$

$$C - S = 40 - 10 = 30$$

$$S \div C = 10 \div 40 = \frac{1}{4}$$

None of these seem reasonable.

7. D: Since Harlan knows the cost of each bag of carrots, and also how many total carrots he needs, he also needs to know the number of carrots in each bag to find the number of bags he needs to buy. Then, he can multiply the number of bags by the price to find the amount of money the carrots for his stew will cost.

8. A: To solve, test each answer. Notice that in (A), the numerator has been multiplied by 3 to get 12. The denominator has been multiplied by 3 to get 21. In (B) the numerator has been multiplied by 4 and the denominator has been multiplied by 5. In (C), the numerator has been multiplied by 3 and the denominator has been multiplied by 4. In (D), the numerator has been multiplied by 4 and the denominator has been multiplied by a number less than 4.

9. C: Aaron ran four miles from home and then back again, so he ran a total of eight miles. Therefore, statement III is false. Statements I and II, however, are both true. Since Aaron ran eight miles in eighty minutes, he ran an average of one mile every ten minutes, or six miles per hour; he ran two miles from point A to B in 20 minutes and four miles from D to E in 40 minutes, so his running speed between both sets of points was the same.

10. B: The total number of Evercell batteries is $(4 \times E)$ and the total number of Durapower batteries is $(6 \times D)$. The sum of the two is the total number of batteries in the store.

11. A: To solve, first figure out how much room is left when her car and the garage are taken into account: 19 feet – 15 feet = 4 feet. To center the car, it would have to be parked 2 feet from the front of the garage.

12. C: Notice that Set M starts with 1 and increases by adding 3 each time, so the numbers more than 20 in this set are: (22, 25, 28, 31, …) Set V is the set of odd numbers, so the numbers in this set greater than 20 are: (21, 23, 25, 27, 29, …) The first number common to both sets is 25.

13. D: To solve, isolate the x on one side of the equation.

4x = 36 – 4

4x = 32

x = 8

14. A: $C = \frac{3}{4}(100) + 20$. Since $\frac{1}{4}$ of the original $100 was sent to the savings account, $\frac{3}{4}$ of the money was kept in cash. The bonus was then added afterward.

15. C: The scalene triangle does not have a line of symmetry. The hexagon has two lines of symmetry, the arrow as one line of symmetry and the curve has one line of symmetry.

16. D: There are perpendicular edges at every corner of the cube.

17. C: The fraction of Figure A that is shaded is $\frac{2}{5}$. The fraction of Figure B that is shaded is $\frac{12}{30}$. $\frac{12}{30}$ reduces to $\frac{2}{5}$ by dividing the numerator and denominator by 6. Therefore, fractions of the shaded regions are equal.

18. B: The situation may be modeled with the equation $\frac{1}{3} + \frac{1}{2} = \frac{1}{t}$, which simplifies to $\frac{5}{6} = \frac{1}{t}$. Thus, $t = \frac{6}{5}$. If working together, it will take them 1.2 hours to decorate the cake.

19. A: The simplest way to compare the two pieces of pie is to find a common dominator for both fractions. The older daughter was given 2/5 of the pie, while the younger daughter was given 1/3 of the pie. The least common dominator for the two fractions is 15. Therefore, the older daughter received 6/15 of the pie and the younger daughter received 5/15 of the pie. 6/15 is larger than 5/15; therefore, the older daughter received a larger slice of the pie.

20. C: Since one half of the wealth is being distributed in 5 equal parts, each relative is receiving $\frac{1}{5}$ of the $\frac{1}{2}$. In other words, $\frac{1}{5} \times \frac{1}{2} = \frac{1}{10}$.

21. B: Since 3 items are being purchased and each cost \$3.99, these two numbers must be multiplied. Choice A shows $3 \times 4 - 3 \times 0.01 = 3 \times (4 - 0.01) = 3 \times 3.99$. Choice C shows $3 \times 3 + 3 \times 0.9 + 3 \times 0.09 = 3 \times (3 + 0.9 + 0.09) = 3 \times 3.99$. Choice D shows $3.99 + 3.99 + 3.99 = 3 \times 3.99$. Only choice B shows a different operation: division.

22. D: A line of symmetry is a line where the figure could be folded in half to match up perfectly with itself. Each one of the lines is a line of symmetry because each point on one side of the figure is the same distance from the line of symmetry, and the line segment that can be created by connecting each point with its corresponding point will be perpendicular to the line of symmetry.

23. B: Choice A is a number in the thousandths; D is a number in the hundredths; C and B are in tenths. Four-tenths is the largest of these choices.

24. B: The formula for the area of trapezoids is not necessarily needed here to do this problem. Since the relationship between the area, A, and the height, h, can be seen in the chart, looking at the third and fourth columns to see if there is a pattern will show a relationship between the variables. Each value in the area column is equal to 6 times the value in the height column. So, we get $A = 6h$.

25. A: By adding all of the dimes, we find that there are a total of 100 dimes in the bag. 10 of them were minted in 1945. The probability, then, of choosing a dime minted in 1945 is 10 out of 100, which is equivalent to the fraction $\frac{1}{10}$.

26. D: This procedure first finds the area to be fertilized, by multiplying the length and width of the rectangular yard. Then, it divides that area by the area each pound of fertilizer will cover.

27. C: To answer this question correctly, convert all numbers to decimal form to make them easy to compare. Since two of the numbers are already in decimal form, we only need to convert $1\frac{7}{10}$ and $1\frac{3}{4}$ to decimal form.

$$7 \div 10 = 0.7, \text{ so } 1\frac{7}{10} = 1.7$$

$$\text{and } 3 \div 4 = 0.75, \text{ so } 1\frac{3}{4} = 1.75$$

Therefore, by comparing place values from left to right of 1.7, 1.72, 1.75 and 1.695, we see that 1.695 is least, 1.7 is next greatest, 1.72 is next, and 1.75 is greatest. So, Antonio should buy the border that is $1\frac{3}{4}$ inches wide.

28. D: Only answer D correctly shows each amount of salt being subtracted from the original total amount of 26 ounces that was in the box.

29. A: The box symbol shown at ∠R means that ∠R measures 90°. Since we are told $m\angle S$ is 20° less than $m\angle R$, subtract 90 –20 to get 70. This means that $m\angle S = 70°$. The sum of $m\angle R$ and $m\angle S$ is found by adding: 90 +70 = 160. The sum of all angles in a triangle always adds up to 180°, so subtracting 180 – 160 results in a difference of 20. So, $m\angle T$ is 20°.

30. B: To answer this question, that there are 9 equal-sized panes in the window. Of the 9 panes, 3 have a dark tint and can be represented by the fraction, $\frac{3}{9}$, which is equivalent to $\frac{1}{3}$. 2 of the panes are lightly tinted and can be represented by $\frac{2}{9}$. So, the number sentence, $\frac{1}{3} + \frac{2}{9} = \frac{5}{9}$ best represents the total section of the window which is tinted.

31. B: If each car brought from 1 to 3 people, then 50 is the best estimate of the number of people that could have arrived in the 25 cars. 25 is too low because this would mean only 1 person could have arrived in each car. 75 and 100 are too high, because then this would mean 3 or more people arrived in each car. The answer, 50 people, would mean that each car brought 2 people each, which is the average number of people who arrived per car.

32. D: Note that the ratio asked for is the number of people who ordered milk to the number who ordered juice. The number of people who ordered coffee does not matter here. This compares 10 to 25, and the order is important here. Since the ratio is with the number of people who ordered milk first, the 10 must come first. So, the ratio is 10 to 25, but the ratio can be written in simpler form by dividing both numbers in the ratio by 5, to get the ratio: 2 to 5.

33. C: Looking at the chart, a pattern can be seen in the relationship between the number of gills and the number of fluid ounces. Each number of gills in the first column, when multiplied by 4, gives the number of fluid ounces in the second column. So, f equals 4 times g, or $f = 4g$.

34. D: The amount charged for miles hauled will require us to multiply the number of miles by $0.05. The charge for each load of $80 is not changed by the number of miles hauled. That will be added to the amount charged for miles hauled. So, the equation needs to show 0.05 times miles plus 80, or $c = 0.05m + 80$.

35. B: A cube has six square faces. The arrangement of these faces in a two-dimensional figure is a net of a cube if the figure can be folded to form a cube. If this is folded, the bottom square in the second column will overlap the fourth square in the top row, so the figure does not represent a net of a cube. The other figures represent three of the eleven possible nets of a cube.

36. B: A right angle has a measure of 90 degrees, which is greater than the measure of an acute angle, with an angle less than 90 degrees. A right angle also has a measure less than the measure of an obtuse angle, which has a measure greater than 90 degrees.

37. C: The pattern in the table is that the number of customers is increasing by 25 each week. This means that there should be $205 + 25 = 230$ customers expected in week 4.

Week	Customers
1	155
2	180
3	205
4	230

+25

+25

+25

38. D: There are 12 even-numbered floors between floors 1 and 25. At each one, the elevator gains 2 people, for a net gain of 24. There are 11 odd-numbered floors between floors 1 and 25 (not counting floors 1 and 25). At each one, the elevator loses 1 person, for a net loss of 11. The elevator leaves the first floor with 3 people, so the total arriving at the 25th floor is 3 + 24 – 11 = 16.

Section 3: Reading Comprehension

1. A: If someone is "elated", they are extremely happy and excited about something.

2. D: The first sentence of paragraph 2 uses a simile when it says Scott "stood like a statue." A simile uses "like" or "as" to compare one thing to another.

3. B: Choice B most clearly and completely expresses the theme of the story. Coach Travis tells Scott that "it's all about perspective", and then says that how Scott decides to look at it is up to him.

4. C: Choice C is the most complete and accurate summary of the story overall. A, B, and D are incorrect because they cover only part of the story or some of the main ideas and concepts.

5. A: Scott is upset in the story because he feels responsible for the team's loss.

6. B: is the best choice because the main purpose of dance in Native American culture is to communicate a message. A, C, and D are not the best choices because they do not accurately reflect the main purpose of dance in Native American culture.

7. A: is the best choice because the Iroquois corn husk dance and the Hopi Snake Ceremonial were both intended to bring good crops. B, C, and D are not the best choices because they do not represent the purpose of these dances.

8. D: is the best choice because it is the only statement of fact. A, B, and C are not the best choices because they are all statements of opinion.

9. C: is the best choice because in many Native American tribes the eagle feather represents strength. A, B, and D are not the best choices because they do not reflect the meaning of the eagle feather in many Native American tribes.

10. A: is the best choice because the author's main purpose in writing this article is to inform the reader. B, C, and D are not the best choices because the author's primary purpose in writing this article is not to entertain, to influence, or to persuade.

11. B: You may already know that a conifer is a type of tree. If you do not know this, you can deduce the information based on the fact that the word is used in the description of the Giant Sequoia tree.

12. D: In the first sentence, the passage states that *most* people think the Giant Sequoia is the largest organism. It goes on to explain that there are some people who do not agree.

13. C: The first paragraph describes the General Sherman as the largest Giant Sequoia. The other answer choices include words that can be found in the passage.

14. C: Look at lines 17–23 to find the answer. The passage explains that goldenrod flowers and aspen groves are connected with underground root systems, leading some people to believe that these organisms are bigger than Giant Sequoia trees.

15. D: The passage gives the diameter of the tree at the bottom, but the diameter at the top is not given. You cannot assume the answer, so there is no way to know what the diameter is given the data in the passage.

16. C: is the best choice because the official name of the Alamo is San Antonio de Valero. A, B, and D are not the best choices because they list incorrect official names for the Alamo.

17. A: is the best choice because the author's purpose in writing "Remember the Alamo" is clearly to inform. B, C, and D are not the best choices because they represent inaccurate purposes for the story.

18. D: is the best choice because freedom was the main motivation for those who fought at the Alamo. A, B, and C are not the best choices because they do not portray the primary motivation for the Alamo fighters.

19. B: is the best choice because the Alamo was designed to serve many purposes in the community. A, C, and D are not the best choices because they do not reflect the real purpose behind the design of the Alamo.

20. D: is the best choice because it is a statement of opinion. A, B, and C are not the best choices because they are all statements of fact.

21. B: The passage gives general instructions for tomato plant culture from seeding to providing support for the vines. Answers A and D are too specific, focusing on details of the text. Answer C is too general: the passage does not fully describe how to operate a farm.

22. C: The passage states that seeds germinated in late March will be ready for the garden after the last frost.

23. A: The passage states that seeds germinated in late March will be ready for the garden after the last frost, implying that exposure to freezing temperatures would harm them.

24. A: The text states that pinching the bud is done to make the plants stronger.

25. D: Although all the other answers make mention of information contained in the paragraph, the overall purpose of this paragraph is as stated, to describe the support procedure.

Section 4: Mathematics Achievement

1. C: Add the 1 hour and 30 minutes to find that Janice finishes her homework at 4:15 PM. Next, add 1 hour and 45 minutes to find that Janice returns home at 6:00 PM.

2. A: The digit 5 is in the 5th column, which is the ten thousands column. Therefore, the digit represents the value 50,000.

3. C: The value of each number in the pattern is a multiple of 100. Therefore, the 14th number represents the value of the product of 14 and 100; $14 \times 100 = 1400$.

4. D: The recipe is being multiplied by 4 in this problem, therefore $\frac{1}{8} = \frac{4}{32}$ so a total of 4 cups of milk are needed. Since this is not one of the choices, a conversion is needed. 1 pint = 2 cups and 1 quart = 2 pints, therefore 1 quart = 4 cups.

5. C: This is a simple subtraction problem involving money. $25 -$18 = $7

6. A: To find the difference, subtract. It is important to align decimal places. Note, when subtracting here, the digit in the hundredths place in 0.33 has no digit aligned above it. We must add a zero to 1.5 so that we can align the hundredths places correctly. Now we can subtract 33 hundredths from the 50 hundredths to get 17 hundredths. So, we get 1.17 as our correct answer.

7. C: This is a simple addition problem. Line up the decimals so that they are all in the same place in the equation, and see that there is a 3 by itself in the hundredths column. Then add the tenths column: 6+3+5 to get 14. Write down the 4 and carry the 1. Add the ones column: 3 plus the carried 1. Write down 4. Then write down the 1.

8. A: Multiply 24 by 4 to get 96 and multiply 12 by 6 to get 72. Then, add 96 and 72 to get the correct answer, 168.

9. C: To solve this formula, follow the order of operations. First, add what is in the parenthesis, 4 + 2, to get 6. Then, multiply the 6 by 35 to get 210. Last, we should add 20 + 210 + 47 to get 277.

10. B: Write 606, then add the decimal in the thousandths place, the third place from the right.

11. B: There are 2 green sections on the spinner and the spinner has 6 sections in all. The probability of spinning green is 2 out of 6, when expressed as a fraction is $\frac{2}{6}$. Written in simplest terms, the fraction is $\frac{1}{3}$.

12. C: The number line is divided into tenths. Thus, between the whole numbers, 5 and 6, lie the decimals, 5.1, 5.2, 5.3, 5.4, 5.5, 5.6, 5.7, 5.8, and 5.9. Point P represents the decimal, 5.8.

13. B: By changing the mixed numbers into improper fractions, $4\frac{1}{3} - 2\frac{2}{3}$ becomes $\frac{13}{3} - \frac{8}{3} = \frac{5}{3}$. Changing $\frac{5}{3}$ back into a mixed number yields $1\frac{2}{3}$.

14. D: The mean is just the average. To calculate this, find the total of all 10 numbers by adding. Then, divide that total by 10 because that is the number of data points. The total is 750, so the mean of this group of numbers is 75.

15. B: To answer this question, find the total number of bulbs required by multiplying 10 by 3. The number of packages of bulbs required can be found by dividing this total number of bulbs, 30, by 5, to find that 6 packages are needed. Then, multiplying 6 by the cost per package, 8, we find that the total cost for all the bulbs needed was $48.

16. C: First, find the least common denominator: $\frac{4\times16}{5\times16} - \frac{1\times5}{16\times5} = \frac{64}{80} - \frac{5}{80}$, then subtract the numerators: $\frac{64}{80} - \frac{5}{80} = \frac{59}{80}$. To find where this answer lies on the number line, consider that $0 = \frac{0}{80}$, $\frac{1}{4} = \frac{20}{80}$, $\frac{1}{2} = \frac{40}{80}$, $\frac{3}{4} = \frac{60}{80}$, and $1 = \frac{80}{80}$. So $\frac{59}{80}$ is between $\frac{40}{80} = \frac{1}{2}$ and $\frac{60}{80} = \frac{3}{4}$.

17. C: The right triangle is being rotated 90 degrees in a clockwise direction about the vertex point $(2, 5)$.

18. B: The value of A is 5,032,080; the value of C is 5,320,008; and the value of D is 5,328. B shows 5,320,080 which is the original number.

19. C: To round to the thousands place, look at the digit to the right (in the hundreds place). If that digit is 4 or less, leave the digit in the thousands place; if that digit is 5 or more, add one to the digit in the thousands place.

20. A: Use the volume of a rectangular prism formula $V = L \times W \times H$ to determine the length of the tank.

$$200 = L \times 8 \times 5 \rightarrow 200 = 40L \rightarrow L = 5 \text{ feet.}$$

21. C: The approximate price of the fence is found by rounding to 70 feet at $4 per foot. $P = 70 \times \$4 = \$280$. The actual price is $P = 71 \times \$3.98 = \$282.58$.

22. A: Translate the point 5 units to the right and 4 units down to find the location of the lighthouse.

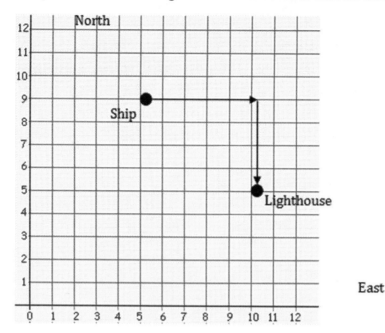

23. B: A regular pentagon is a 5-sided figure with all sides equal in length. Therefore, the perimeter is $5 \times 6.5 = 32.5$ centimeters.

24. B: There are 3 feet in every yard. Since we are converting from a larger unit to a smaller unit, we should multiply the number of the larger unit by the conversion factor. That is 120 times 3 equals 360.

25. D: To answer this question, note that the fractions have common denominators. When adding fractions with common denominators, we need to add only the numerators, so, the sum of $\frac{6}{10}$ and $\frac{8}{10}$ is $\frac{14}{10}$. This should then be written as a mixed number, $1\frac{4}{10}$, which is found by dividing 14 by 10, which gives the whole number and the remainder becomes your new numerator over the same denominator of 10. The fraction $\frac{4}{10}$ can also be written as $\frac{2}{5}$ by dividing numerator and denominator by the common factor of 2. Therefore, $\frac{14}{10}$ is equivalent to $1\frac{2}{5}$. Be careful here to remember the 1 from the original $1\frac{6}{10}$ amount given in the problem, which must be added to the $1\frac{2}{5}$ to make a total of $2\frac{2}{5}$.

26. B: By the definition of an isosceles trapezoid, the legs (non-parallel sides) are congruent. Since the figure is defined as an isosceles, it is known that $\overline{PS}$ and $\overline{QR}$ are parallel and not congruent in length.

27. B: To simplify this expression, use the order of operations. First, do what is in the parenthesis and subtract 1 from 3 to get 2. Then, we multiply 4 times 2 to get 8. Last, subtract the 8 from 40 to get 32.

28. B: One method that can be used to answer this question is to write and solve the proportion: $\frac{3}{20} = \frac{V}{360}$, where V stands for the number of Brand V televisions that were sold at the furniture store. To solve the proportion, we can cross multiply: 20 times V and 3 times 360, which gives the equation: $20V = 1{,}080$. We solve this equation by dividing both sides of the equation by 20 to get $V = 54$.

29. B: The water temperature increased by about 2° every 3 minutes, or $\frac{2}{3}$ of a degree every minute. Multiplying the increase in degrees per minute by the total number of minutes yields

$$\frac{2°}{3 \text{ min}} \times 20 \text{ min} = \frac{40}{3}, \text{ or } 13.33°$$

Since the problem asks for the increase in temperature and not the total temperature that results after the increases, 13 is the closest to our answer.

30. C: When subtraction comes before division, it must be placed in parentheses. The phrase "subtract 4 from 18" means the same as "18 minus 4."

How to Overcome Test Anxiety

Just the thought of taking a test is enough to make most people a little nervous. A test is an important event that can have a long-term impact on your future, so it's important to take it seriously and it's natural to feel anxious about performing well. But just because anxiety is normal, that doesn't mean that it's helpful in test taking, or that you should simply accept it as part of your life. Anxiety can have a variety of effects. These effects can be mild, like making you feel slightly nervous, or severe, like blocking your ability to focus or remember even a simple detail.

If you experience test anxiety—whether severe or mild—it's important to know how to beat it. To discover this, first you need to understand what causes test anxiety.

Causes of Test Anxiety

While we often think of anxiety as an uncontrollable emotional state, it can actually be caused by simple, practical things. One of the most common causes of test anxiety is that a person does not feel adequately prepared for their test. This feeling can be the result of many different issues such as poor study habits or lack of organization, but the most common culprit is time management. Starting to study too late, failing to organize your study time to cover all of the material, or being distracted while you study will mean that you're not well prepared for the test. This may lead to cramming the night before, which will cause you to be physically and mentally exhausted for the test. Poor time management also contributes to feelings of stress, fear, and hopelessness as you realize you are not well prepared but don't know what to do about it.

Other times, test anxiety is not related to your preparation for the test but comes from unresolved fear. This may be a past failure on a test, or poor performance on tests in general. It may come from comparing yourself to others who seem to be performing better or from the stress of living up to expectations. Anxiety may be driven by fears of the future—how failure on this test would affect your educational and career goals. These fears are often completely irrational, but they can still negatively impact your test performance.

> **Review Video: 3 Reasons You Have Test Anxiety**
> Visit mometrix.com/academy and enter code: 428468

Elements of Test Anxiety

As mentioned earlier, test anxiety is considered to be an emotional state, but it has physical and mental components as well. Sometimes you may not even realize that you are suffering from test anxiety until you notice the physical symptoms. These can include trembling hands, rapid heartbeat, sweating, nausea, and tense muscles. Extreme anxiety may lead to fainting or vomiting. Obviously, any of these symptoms can have a negative impact on testing. It is important to recognize them as soon as they begin to occur so that you can address the problem before it damages your performance.

> **Review Video: 3 Ways to Tell You Have Test Anxiety**
> Visit mometrix.com/academy and enter code: 927847

The mental components of test anxiety include trouble focusing and inability to remember learned information. During a test, your mind is on high alert, which can help you recall information and stay focused for an extended period of time. However, anxiety interferes with your mind's natural processes, causing you to blank out, even on the questions you know well. The strain of testing during anxiety makes it difficult to stay focused, especially on a test that may take several hours. Extreme anxiety can take a huge mental toll, making it difficult not only to recall test information but even to understand the test questions or pull your thoughts together.

> **Review Video: How Test Anxiety Affects Memory**
> Visit mometrix.com/academy and enter code: 609003

Effects of Test Anxiety

Test anxiety is like a disease—if left untreated, it will get progressively worse. Anxiety leads to poor performance, and this reinforces the feelings of fear and failure, which in turn lead to poor performances on subsequent tests. It can grow from a mild nervousness to a crippling condition. If allowed to progress, test anxiety can have a big impact on your schooling, and consequently on your future.

Test anxiety can spread to other parts of your life. Anxiety on tests can become anxiety in any stressful situation, and blanking on a test can turn into panicking in a job situation. But fortunately, you don't have to let anxiety rule your testing and determine your grades. There are a number of relatively simple steps you can take to move past anxiety and function normally on a test and in the rest of life.

> **Review Video: How Test Anxiety Impacts Your Grades**
> Visit mometrix.com/academy and enter code: 939819

Physical Steps for Beating Test Anxiety

While test anxiety is a serious problem, the good news is that it can be overcome. It doesn't have to control your ability to think and remember information. While it may take time, you can begin taking steps today to beat anxiety.

Just as your first hint that you may be struggling with anxiety comes from the physical symptoms, the first step to treating it is also physical. Rest is crucial for having a clear, strong mind. If you are tired, it is much easier to give in to anxiety. But if you establish good sleep habits, your body and mind will be ready to perform optimally, without the strain of exhaustion. Additionally, sleeping well helps you to retain information better, so you're more likely to recall the answers when you see the test questions.

Getting good sleep means more than going to bed on time. It's important to allow your brain time to relax. Take study breaks from time to time so it doesn't get overworked, and don't study right before bed. Take time to rest your mind before trying to rest your body, or you may find it difficult to fall asleep.

> **Review Video: <u>The Importance of Sleep for Your Brain</u>**
> Visit mometrix.com/academy and enter code: 319338

Along with sleep, other aspects of physical health are important in preparing for a test. Good nutrition is vital for good brain function. Sugary foods and drinks may give a burst of energy but this burst is followed by a crash, both physically and emotionally. Instead, fuel your body with protein and vitamin-rich foods.

Also, drink plenty of water. Dehydration can lead to headaches and exhaustion, especially if your brain is already under stress from the rigors of the test. Particularly if your test is a long one, drink water during the breaks. And if possible, take an energy-boosting snack to eat between sections.

> **Review Video: <u>How Diet Can Affect your Mood</u>**
> Visit mometrix.com/academy and enter code: 624317

Along with sleep and diet, a third important part of physical health is exercise. Maintaining a steady workout schedule is helpful, but even taking 5-minute study breaks to walk can help get your blood pumping faster and clear your head. Exercise also releases endorphins, which contribute to a positive feeling and can help combat test anxiety.

When you nurture your physical health, you are also contributing to your mental health. If your body is healthy, your mind is much more likely to be healthy as well. So take time to rest, nourish your body with healthy food and water, and get moving as much as possible. Taking these physical steps will make you stronger and more able to take the mental steps necessary to overcome test anxiety.

> **Review Video: <u>How to Stay Healthy and Prevent Test Anxiety</u>**
> Visit mometrix.com/academy and enter code: 877894

Mental Steps for Beating Test Anxiety

Working on the mental side of test anxiety can be more challenging, but as with the physical side, there are clear steps you can take to overcome it. As mentioned earlier, test anxiety often stems from lack of preparation, so the obvious solution is to prepare for the test. Effective studying may be the most important weapon you have for beating test anxiety, but you can and should employ several other mental tools to combat fear.

First, boost your confidence by reminding yourself of past success—tests or projects that you aced. If you're putting as much effort into preparing for this test as you did for those, there's no reason you should expect to fail here. Work hard to prepare; then trust your preparation.

Second, surround yourself with encouraging people. It can be helpful to find a study group, but be sure that the people you're around will encourage a positive attitude. If you spend time with others who are anxious or cynical, this will only contribute to your own anxiety. Look for others who are motivated to study hard from a desire to succeed, not from a fear of failure.

Third, reward yourself. A test is physically and mentally tiring, even without anxiety, and it can be helpful to have something to look forward to. Plan an activity following the test, regardless of the outcome, such as going to a movie or getting ice cream.

When you are taking the test, if you find yourself beginning to feel anxious, remind yourself that you know the material. Visualize successfully completing the test. Then take a few deep, relaxing breaths and return to it. Work through the questions carefully but with confidence, knowing that you are capable of succeeding.

Developing a healthy mental approach to test taking will also aid in other areas of life. Test anxiety affects more than just the actual test—it can be damaging to your mental health and even contribute to depression. It's important to beat test anxiety before it becomes a problem for more than testing.

> **Review Video: Test Anxiety and Depression**
> Visit mometrix.com/academy and enter code: 904704

Study Strategy

Being prepared for the test is necessary to combat anxiety, but what does being prepared look like? You may study for hours on end and still not feel prepared. What you need is a strategy for test prep. The next few pages outline our recommended steps to help you plan out and conquer the challenge of preparation.

STEP 1: SCOPE OUT THE TEST

Learn everything you can about the format (multiple choice, essay, etc.) and what will be on the test. Gather any study materials, course outlines, or sample exams that may be available. Not only will this help you to prepare, but knowing what to expect can help to alleviate test anxiety.

STEP 2: MAP OUT THE MATERIAL

Look through the textbook or study guide and make note of how many chapters or sections it has. Then divide these over the time you have. For example, if a book has 15 chapters and you have five days to study, you need to cover three chapters each day. Even better, if you have the time, leave an extra day at the end for overall review after you have gone through the material in depth.

If time is limited, you may need to prioritize the material. Look through it and make note of which sections you think you already have a good grasp on, and which need review. While you are studying, skim quickly through the familiar sections and take more time on the challenging parts. Write out your plan so you don't get lost as you go. Having a written plan also helps you feel more in control of the study, so anxiety is less likely to arise from feeling overwhelmed at the amount to cover.

STEP 3: GATHER YOUR TOOLS

Decide what study method works best for you. Do you prefer to highlight in the book as you study and then go back over the highlighted portions? Or do you type out notes of the important information? Or is it helpful to make flashcards that you can carry with you? Assemble the pens, index cards, highlighters, post-it notes, and any other materials you may need so you won't be distracted by getting up to find things while you study.

If you're having a hard time retaining the information or organizing your notes, experiment with different methods. For example, try color-coding by subject with colored pens, highlighters, or post-it notes. If you learn better by hearing, try recording yourself reading your notes so you can listen while in the car, working out, or simply sitting at your desk. Ask a friend to quiz you from your flashcards, or try teaching someone the material to solidify it in your mind.

STEP 4: CREATE YOUR ENVIRONMENT

It's important to avoid distractions while you study. This includes both the obvious distractions like visitors and the subtle distractions like an uncomfortable chair (or a too-comfortable couch that makes you want to fall asleep). Set up the best study environment possible: good lighting and a comfortable work area. If background music helps you focus, you may want to turn it on, but otherwise keep the room quiet. If you are using a computer to take notes, be sure you don't have any other windows open, especially applications like social media, games, or anything else that could distract you. Silence your phone and turn off notifications. Be sure to keep water close by so you stay hydrated while you study (but avoid unhealthy drinks and snacks).

Also, take into account the best time of day to study. Are you freshest first thing in the morning? Try to set aside some time then to work through the material. Is your mind clearer in the afternoon or evening? Schedule your study session then. Another method is to study at the same time of day that you will take the test, so that your brain gets used to working on the material at that time and will be ready to focus at test time.

STEP 5: STUDY!

Once you have done all the study preparation, it's time to settle into the actual studying. Sit down, take a few moments to settle your mind so you can focus, and begin to follow your study plan. Don't give in to distractions or let yourself procrastinate. This is your time to prepare so you'll be ready to fearlessly approach the test. Make the most of the time and stay focused.

Of course, you don't want to burn out. If you study too long you may find that you're not retaining the information very well. Take regular study breaks. For example, taking five minutes out of every hour to walk briskly, breathing deeply and swinging your arms, can help your mind stay fresh.

As you get to the end of each chapter or section, it's a good idea to do a quick review. Remind yourself of what you learned and work on any difficult parts. When you feel that you've mastered the material, move on to the next part. At the end of your study session, briefly skim through your notes again.

But while review is helpful, cramming last minute is NOT. If at all possible, work ahead so that you won't need to fit all your study into the last day. Cramming overloads your brain with more information than it can process and retain, and your tired mind may struggle to recall even previously learned information when it is overwhelmed with last-minute study. Also, the urgent nature of cramming and the stress placed on your brain contribute to anxiety. You'll be more likely to go to the test feeling unprepared and having trouble thinking clearly.

So don't cram, and don't stay up late before the test, even just to review your notes at a leisurely pace. Your brain needs rest more than it needs to go over the information again. In fact, plan to finish your studies by noon or early afternoon the day before the test. Give your brain the rest of the day to relax or focus on other things, and get a good night's sleep. Then you will be fresh for the test and better able to recall what you've studied.

STEP 6: TAKE A PRACTICE TEST

Many courses offer sample tests, either online or in the study materials. This is an excellent resource to check whether you have mastered the material, as well as to prepare for the test format and environment.

Check the test format ahead of time: the number of questions, the type (multiple choice, free response, etc.), and the time limit. Then create a plan for working through them. For example, if you have 30 minutes to take a 60-question test, your limit is 30 seconds per question. Spend less time on the questions you know well so that you can take more time on the difficult ones.

If you have time to take several practice tests, take the first one open book, with no time limit. Work through the questions at your own pace and make sure you fully understand them. Gradually work up to taking a test under test conditions: sit at a desk with all study materials put away and set a timer. Pace yourself to make sure you finish the test with time to spare and go back to check your answers if you have time.

After each test, check your answers. On the questions you missed, be sure you understand why you missed them. Did you misread the question (tests can use tricky wording)? Did you forget the information? Or was it something you hadn't learned? Go back and study any shaky areas that the practice tests reveal.

Taking these tests not only helps with your grade, but also aids in combating test anxiety. If you're already used to the test conditions, you're less likely to worry about it, and working through tests until you're scoring well gives you a confidence boost. Go through the practice tests until you feel comfortable, and then you can go into the test knowing that you're ready for it.

Test Tips

On test day, you should be confident, knowing that you've prepared well and are ready to answer the questions. But aside from preparation, there are several test day strategies you can employ to maximize your performance.

First, as stated before, get a good night's sleep the night before the test (and for several nights before that, if possible). Go into the test with a fresh, alert mind rather than staying up late to study.

Try not to change too much about your normal routine on the day of the test. It's important to eat a nutritious breakfast, but if you normally don't eat breakfast at all, consider eating just a protein bar. If you're a coffee drinker, go ahead and have your normal coffee. Just make sure you time it so that the caffeine doesn't wear off right in the middle of your test. Avoid sugary beverages, and drink enough water to stay hydrated but not so much that you need a restroom break 10 minutes into the test. If your test isn't first thing in the morning, consider going for a walk or doing a light workout before the test to get your blood flowing.

Allow yourself enough time to get ready, and leave for the test with plenty of time to spare so you won't have the anxiety of scrambling to arrive in time. Another reason to be early is to select a good seat. It's helpful to sit away from doors and windows, which can be distracting. Find a good seat, get out your supplies, and settle your mind before the test begins.

When the test begins, start by going over the instructions carefully, even if you already know what to expect. Make sure you avoid any careless mistakes by following the directions.

Then begin working through the questions, pacing yourself as you've practiced. If you're not sure on an answer, don't spend too much time on it, and don't let it shake your confidence. Either skip it and come back later, or eliminate as many wrong answers as possible and guess among the remaining ones. Don't dwell on these questions as you continue—put them out of your mind and focus on what lies ahead.

Be sure to read all of the answer choices, even if you're sure the first one is the right answer. Sometimes you'll find a better one if you keep reading. But don't second-guess yourself if you do immediately know the answer. Your gut instinct is usually right. Don't let test anxiety rob you of the information you know.

If you have time at the end of the test (and if the test format allows), go back and review your answers. Be cautious about changing any, since your first instinct tends to be correct, but make sure you didn't misread any of the questions or accidentally mark the wrong answer choice. Look over any you skipped and make an educated guess.

At the end, leave the test feeling confident. You've done your best, so don't waste time worrying about your performance or wishing you could change anything. Instead, celebrate the successful completion of this test. And finally, use this test to learn how to deal with anxiety even better next time.

Important Qualification

Not all anxiety is created equal. If your test anxiety is causing major issues in your life beyond the classroom or testing center, or if you are experiencing troubling physical symptoms related to your anxiety, it may be a sign of a serious physiological or psychological condition. If this sounds like your situation, we strongly encourage you to seek professional help.

How to Overcome Your Fear of Math

The word *math* is enough to strike fear into most hearts. How many of us have memories of sitting through confusing lectures, wrestling over mind-numbing homework, or taking tests that still seem incomprehensible even after hours of study? Years after graduation, many still shudder at these memories.

The fact is, math is not just a classroom subject. It has real-world implications that you face every day, whether you realize it or not. This may be balancing your monthly budget, deciding how many supplies to buy for a project, or simply splitting a meal check with friends. The idea of daily confrontations with math can be so paralyzing that some develop a condition known as *math anxiety*.

But you do NOT need to be paralyzed by this anxiety! In fact, while you may have thought all your life that you're not good at math, or that your brain isn't wired to understand it, the truth is that you may have been conditioned to think this way. From your earliest school days, the way you were taught affected the way you viewed different subjects. And the way math has been taught has changed.

Several decades ago, there was a shift in American math classrooms. The focus changed from traditional problem-solving to a conceptual view of topics, de-emphasizing the importance of learning the basics and building on them. The solid foundation necessary for math progression and confidence was undermined. Math became more of a vague concept than a concrete idea. Today, it is common to think of math, not as a straightforward system, but as a mysterious, complicated method that can't be fully understood unless you're a genius.

This is why you may still have nightmares about being called on to answer a difficult problem in front of the class. Math anxiety is a very real, though unnecessary, fear.

Math anxiety may begin with a single class period. Let's say you missed a day in 6th grade math and never quite understood the concept that was taught while you were gone. Since math is cumulative, with each new concept building on past ones, this could very well affect the rest of your math career. Without that one day's knowledge, it will be difficult to understand any other concepts that link to it. Rather than realizing that you're just missing one key piece, you may begin to believe that you're simply not capable of understanding math.

This belief can change the way you approach other classes, career options, and everyday life experiences, if you become anxious at the thought that math might be required. A student who loves science may choose a different path of study upon realizing that multiple math classes will be required for a degree. An aspiring medical student may hesitate at the thought of going through the necessary math classes. For some this anxiety escalates into a more extreme state known as *math phobia*.

Math anxiety is challenging to address because it is rooted deeply and may come from a variety of causes: an embarrassing moment in class, a teacher who did not explain concepts well and contributed to a shaky foundation, or a failed test that contributed to the belief of math failure.

These causes add up over time, encouraged by society's popular view that math is hard and unpleasant. Eventually a person comes to firmly believe that he or she is simply bad at math. This belief makes it difficult to grasp new concepts or even remember old ones. Homework and test

114

grades begin to slip, which only confirms the belief. The poor performance is not due to lack of ability but is caused by math anxiety.

Math anxiety is an emotional issue, not a lack of intelligence. But when it becomes deeply rooted, it can become more than just an emotional problem. Physical symptoms appear. Blood pressure may rise and heartbeat may quicken at the sight of a math problem – or even the thought of math! This fear leads to a mental block. When someone with math anxiety is asked to perform a calculation, even a basic problem can seem overwhelming and impossible. The emotional and physical response to the thought of math prevents the brain from working through it logically.

The more this happens, the more a person's confidence drops, and the more math anxiety is generated. This vicious cycle must be broken!

The first step in breaking the cycle is to go back to very beginning and make sure you really understand the basics of how math works and why it works. It is not enough to memorize rules for multiplication and division. If you don't know WHY these rules work, your foundation will be shaky and you will be at risk of developing a phobia. Understanding mathematical concepts not only promotes confidence and security, but allows you to build on this understanding for new concepts. Additionally, you can solve unfamiliar problems using familiar concepts and processes.

Why is it that students in other countries regularly outperform American students in math? The answer likely boils down to a couple of things: the foundation of mathematical conceptual understanding and societal perception. While students in the US are not expected to *like* or *get* math, in many other nations, students are expected not only to understand math but also to excel at it.

Changing the American view of math that leads to math anxiety is a monumental task. It requires changing the training of teachers nationwide, from kindergarten through high school, so that they learn to teach the *why* behind math and to combat the wrong math views that students may develop. It also involves changing the stigma associated with math, so that it is no longer viewed as unpleasant and incomprehensible. While these are necessary changes, they are challenging and will take time. But in the meantime, math anxiety is not irreversible—it can be faced and defeated, one person at a time.

False Beliefs

One reason math anxiety has taken such hold is that several false beliefs have been created and shared until they became widely accepted. Some of these unhelpful beliefs include the following:

There is only one way to solve a math problem. In the same way that you can choose from different driving routes and still arrive at the same house, you can solve a math problem using different methods and still find the correct answer. A person who understands the reasoning behind math calculations may be able to look at an unfamiliar concept and find the right answer, just by applying logic to the knowledge they already have. This approach may be different than what is taught in the classroom, but it is still valid. Unfortunately, even many teachers view math as a subject where the best course of action is to memorize the rule or process for each problem rather than as a place for students to exercise logic and creativity in finding a solution.

Many people don't have a mind for math. A person who has struggled due to poor teaching or math anxiety may falsely believe that he or she doesn't have the mental capacity to grasp mathematical concepts. Most of the time, this is false. Many people find that when they are relieved of their math anxiety, they have more than enough brainpower to understand math.

Men are naturally better at math than women. Even though research has shown this to be false, many young women still avoid math careers and classes because of their belief that their math abilities are inferior. Many girls have come to believe that math is a male skill and have given up trying to understand or enjoy it.

Counting aids are bad. Something like counting on your fingers or drawing out a problem to visualize it may be frowned on as childish or a crutch, but these devices can help you get a tangible understanding of a problem or a concept.

Sadly, many students buy into these ideologies at an early age. A young girl who enjoys math class may be conditioned to think that she doesn't actually have the brain for it because math is for boys, and may turn her energies to other pursuits, permanently closing the door on a wide range of opportunities. A child who finds the right answer but doesn't follow the teacher's method may believe that he is doing it wrong and isn't good at math. A student who never had a problem with math before may have a poor teacher and become confused, yet believe that the problem is because she doesn't have a mathematical mind.

Students who have bought into these erroneous beliefs quickly begin to add their own anxieties, adapting them to their own personal situations:

I'll never use this in real life. A huge number of people wrongly believe that math is irrelevant outside the classroom. By adopting this mindset, they are handicapping themselves for a life in a mathematical world, as well as limiting their career choices. When they are inevitably faced with real-world math, they are conditioning themselves to respond with anxiety.

I'm not quick enough. While timed tests and quizzes, or even simply comparing yourself with other students in the class, can lead to this belief, speed is not an indicator of skill level. A person can work very slowly yet understand at a deep level.

If I can understand it, it's too easy. People with a low view of their own abilities tend to think that if they are able to grasp a concept, it must be simple. They cannot accept the idea that they are capable of understanding math. This belief will make it harder to learn, no matter how intelligent they are.

I just can't learn this. An overwhelming number of people think this, from young children to adults, and much of the time it is simply not true. But this mindset can turn into a self-fulfilling prophecy that keeps you from exercising and growing your math ability.

The good news is, each of these myths can be debunked. For most people, they are based on emotion and psychology, NOT on actual ability! It will take time, effort, and the desire to change, but change is possible. Even if you have spent years thinking that you don't have the capability to understand math, it is not too late to uncover your true ability and find relief from the anxiety that surrounds math.

Math Strategies

It is important to have a plan of attack to combat math anxiety. There are many useful strategies for pinpointing the fears or myths and eradicating them:

Go back to the basics. For most people, math anxiety stems from a poor foundation. You may think that you have a complete understanding of addition and subtraction, or even decimals and percentages, but make absolutely sure. Learning math is different from learning other subjects. For example, when you learn history, you study various time periods and places and events. It may be important to memorize dates or find out about the lives of famous people. When you move from US history to world history, there will be some overlap, but a large amount of the information will be new. Mathematical concepts, on the other hand, are very closely linked and highly dependent on each other. It's like climbing a ladder – if a rung is missing from your understanding, it may be difficult or impossible for you to climb any higher, no matter how hard you try. So go back and make sure your math foundation is strong. This may mean taking a remedial math course, going to a tutor to work through the shaky concepts, or just going through your old homework to make sure you really understand it.

Speak the language. Math has a large vocabulary of terms and phrases unique to working problems. Sometimes these are completely new terms, and sometimes they are common words, but are used differently in a math setting. If you can't speak the language, it will be very difficult to get a thorough understanding of the concepts. It's common for students to think that they don't understand math when they simply don't understand the vocabulary. The good news is that this is fairly easy to fix. Brushing up on any terms you aren't quite sure of can help bring the rest of the concepts into focus.

Check your anxiety level. When you think about math, do you feel nervous or uncomfortable? Do you struggle with feelings of inadequacy, even on concepts that you know you've already learned? It's important to understand your specific math anxieties, and what triggers them. When you catch yourself falling back on a false belief, mentally replace it with the truth. Don't let yourself believe that you can't learn, or that struggling with a concept means you'll never understand it. Instead, remind yourself of how much you've already learned and dwell on that past success. Visualize grasping the new concept, linking it to your old knowledge, and moving on to the next challenge. Also, learn how to manage anxiety when it arises. There are many techniques for coping with the irrational fears that rise to the surface when you enter the math classroom. This may include controlled breathing, replacing negative thoughts with positive ones, or visualizing success. Anxiety interferes with your ability to concentrate and absorb information, which in turn contributes to greater anxiety. If you can learn how to regain control of your thinking, you will be better able to pay attention, make progress, and succeed!

Don't go it alone. Like any deeply ingrained belief, math anxiety is not easy to eradicate. And there is no need for you to wrestle through it on your own. It will take time, and many people find that speaking with a counselor or psychiatrist helps. They can help you develop strategies for responding to anxiety and overcoming old ideas. Additionally, it can be very helpful to take a short course or seek out a math tutor to help you find and fix the missing rungs on your ladder and make sure that you're ready to progress to the next level. You can also find a number of math aids online: courses that will teach you mental devices for figuring out problems, how to get the most out of your math classes, etc.

Check your math attitude. No matter how much you want to learn and overcome your anxiety, you'll have trouble if you still have a negative attitude toward math. If you think it's too hard, or just have general feelings of dread about math, it will be hard to learn and to break through the anxiety. Work on cultivating a positive math attitude. Remind yourself that math is not just a hurdle to be cleared, but a valuable asset. When you view math with a positive attitude, you'll be much more likely to understand and even enjoy it. This is something you must do for yourself. You may find it helpful to visit with a counselor. Your tutor, friends, and family may cheer you on in your endeavors. But your greatest asset is yourself. You are inside your own mind – tell yourself what you need to hear. Relive past victories. Remind yourself that you are capable of understanding math. Root out any false beliefs that linger and replace them with positive truths. Even if it doesn't feel true at first, it will begin to affect your thinking and pave the way for a positive, anxiety-free mindset.

Aside from these general strategies, there are a number of specific practical things you can do to begin your journey toward overcoming math anxiety. Something as simple as learning a new note-taking strategy can change the way you approach math and give you more confidence and understanding. New study techniques can also make a huge difference.

Math anxiety leads to bad habits. If it causes you to be afraid of answering a question in class, you may gravitate toward the back row. You may be embarrassed to ask for help. And you may procrastinate on assignments, which leads to rushing through them at the last moment when it's too late to get a better understanding. It's important to identify your negative behaviors and replace them with positive ones:

Prepare ahead of time. Read the lesson before you go to class. Being exposed to the topics that will be covered in class ahead of time, even if you don't understand them perfectly, is extremely helpful in increasing what you retain from the lecture. Do your homework and, if you're still shaky, go over some extra problems. The key to a solid understanding of math is practice.

Sit front and center. When you can easily see and hear, you'll understand more, and you'll avoid the distractions of other students if no one is in front of you. Plus, you're more likely to be sitting with students who are positive and engaged, rather than others with math anxiety. Let their positive math attitude rub off on you.

Ask questions in class and out. If you don't understand something, just ask. If you need a more in-depth explanation, the teacher may need to work with you outside of class, but often it's a simple concept you don't quite understand, and a single question may clear it up. If you wait, you may not be able to follow the rest of the day's lesson. For extra help, most professors have office hours outside of class when you can go over concepts one-on-one to clear up any uncertainties. Additionally, there may be a *math lab* or study session you can attend for homework help. Take advantage of this.

Review. Even if you feel that you've fully mastered a concept, review it periodically to reinforce it. Going over an old lesson has several benefits: solidifying your understanding, giving you a confidence boost, and even giving some new insights into material that you're currently learning! Don't let yourself get rusty. That can lead to problems with learning later concepts.

Teaching Tips

While the math student's mindset is the most crucial to overcoming math anxiety, it is also important for others to adjust their math attitudes. Teachers and parents have an enormous influence on how students relate to math. They can either contribute to math confidence or math anxiety.

As a parent or teacher, it is very important to convey a positive math attitude. Retelling horror stories of your own bad experience with math will contribute to a new generation of math anxiety. Even if you don't share your experiences, others will be able to sense your fears and may begin to believe them.

Even a careless comment can have a big impact, so watch for phrases like *He's not good at math* or *I never liked math*. You are a crucial role model, and your children or students will unconsciously adopt your mindset. Give them a positive example to follow. Rather than teaching them to fear the math world before they even know it, teach them about all its potential and excitement.

Work to present math as an integral, beautiful, and understandable part of life. Encourage creativity in solving problems. Watch for false beliefs and dispel them. Cross the lines between subjects: integrate history, English, and music with math. Show students how math is used every day, and how the entire world is based on mathematical principles, from the pull of gravity to the shape of seashells. Instead of letting students see math as a necessary evil, direct them to view it as an imaginative, beautiful art form – an art form that they are capable of mastering and using.

Don't give too narrow a view of math. It is more than just numbers. Yes, working problems and learning formulas is a large part of classroom math. But don't let the teaching stop there. Teach students about the everyday implications of math. Show them how nature works according to the laws of mathematics, and take them outside to make discoveries of their own. Expose them to math-related careers by inviting visiting speakers, asking students to do research and presentations, and learning students' interests and aptitudes on a personal level.

Demonstrate the importance of math. Many people see math as nothing more than a required stepping stone to their degree, a nuisance with no real usefulness. Teach students that algebra is used every day in managing their bank accounts, in following recipes, and in scheduling the day's events. Show them how learning to do geometric proofs helps them to develop logical thinking, an invaluable life skill. Let them see that math surrounds them and is integrally linked to their daily lives: that weather predictions are based on math, that math was used to design cars and other machines, etc. Most of all, give them the tools to use math to enrich their lives.

Make math as tangible as possible. Use visual aids and objects that can be touched. It is much easier to grasp a concept when you can hold it in your hands and manipulate it, rather than just listening to the lecture. Encourage math outside of the classroom. The real world is full of measuring, counting, and calculating, so let students participate in this. Keep your eyes open for numbers and patterns to discuss. Talk about how scores are calculated in sports games and how far apart plants are placed in a garden row for maximum growth. Build the mindset that math is a normal and interesting part of daily life.

Finally, find math resources that help to build a positive math attitude. There are a number of books that show math as fascinating and exciting while teaching important concepts, for example: *The Math Curse; A Wrinkle in Time; The Phantom Tollbooth;* and *Fractals, Googols and Other Mathematical Tales*. You can also find a number of online resources: math puzzles and games, videos that show math in nature, and communities of math enthusiasts. On a local level, students can compete in a variety of math competitions with other schools or join a math club.

The student who experiences math as exciting and interesting is unlikely to suffer from math anxiety. Going through life without this handicap is an immense advantage and opens many doors that others have closed through their fear.

Self-Check

Whether you suffer from math anxiety or not, chances are that you have been exposed to some of the false beliefs mentioned above. Now is the time to check yourself for any errors you may have accepted. Do you think you're not wired for math? Or that you don't need to understand it since you're not planning on a math career? Do you think math is just too difficult for the average person?

Find the errors you've taken to heart and replace them with positive thinking. Are you capable of learning math? Yes! Can you control your anxiety? Yes! These errors will resurface from time to time, so be watchful. Don't let others with math anxiety influence you or sway your confidence. If you're having trouble with a concept, find help. Don't let it discourage you!

Create a plan of attack for defeating math anxiety and sharpening your skills. Do some research and decide if it would help you to take a class, get a tutor, or find some online resources to fine-tune your knowledge. Make the effort to get good nutrition, hydration, and sleep so that you are operating at full capacity. Remind yourself daily that you are skilled and that anxiety does not control you. Your mind is capable of so much more than you know. Give it the tools it needs to grow and thrive.

Tell Us Your Story

We at Mometrix would like to extend our heartfelt thanks to you for letting us be a part of your journey. It is an honor to serve people from all walks of life, people like you, who are committed to building the best future they can for themselves.

We know that each person's situation is unique. But we also know that, whether you are a young student or a mother of four, you care about working to make your own life and the lives of those around you better.

That's why we want to hear your story.

We want to know why you're taking this test. We want to know about the trials you've gone through to get here. And we want to know about the successes you've experienced after taking and passing your test.

SCAN HERE

In addition to your story, which can be an inspiration both to us and to others, we value your feedback. We want to know both what you loved about our book and what you think we can improve on.

The team at Mometrix would be absolutely thrilled to hear from you! So please, send us an email at tellusyourstory@mometrix.com or visit us at mometrix.com/tellusyourstory.php and let's stay in touch.

Additional Bonus Material

Due to our efforts to try to keep this book to a manageable length, we've created a link that will give you access to all of your additional bonus material.

Please visit http://www.mometrix.com/bonus948/iseelower to access the information.

Made in the USA
Columbia, SC
27 August 2023

22162429R00072